FLORA DELANEY

Mastering Space Planning

W

**WATERFORD
& HOWELL**
PUBLISHING

Endorsement Disclaimer

First edition

ISBN: 979-8-9912261-2-7

This book was professionally typeset on Reedsy.
Find out more at reedsy.com

Contents

Publisher's Cataloging-in-Publication Data   vi

Dedication   viii

Why Read This Book   ix

The Power of Space Planning   1

  Space Planning Power in Action   5

  A Look Ahead   9

Floor Planning - Mastering The Design   14

  The Blueprint versus The Floorplan   15

  The Layers of a Floor Plan   17

  The difference is the data   22

  The Problems with the Space Denominator   24

  Basic Floor Planning Designs   28

  The Fundamentals of Floor Planning   34

  Prototypes and Templates   37

Influencing Shoppers - Mastering The Psychology   39

  Six Shopping Trips   41

  Customer Decision Trees   44

  Shopper Centric Merchandising   48

Visual Merchandising – Mastering The Art   51

  Solving Customer Problems   51

  Attractive Organization   54

  Merchandising in the Real World   59

Category Management– Mastering The Process   65

  The Assortment Handoff   70

  Organizational Alignment and POG Processes   76

  The Golden POG and the Planogram Lifecycle   79

Planogram Change Tactics 84

The Combination Planogram Dilemma 88

Off Cycle Changes 92

The Pricing Handoff 93

Next Level Collaboration: Your Supplier Partners 95

Next Level Collaboration: Your Store Partners 99

Planogram Mock-ups 105

Technology - Mastering The Systems 109

What It Takes to Succeed 109

How systems fit together 118

Critical Integrations for Space Systems 121

The Space System as Foundational Data 122

The Space System Conversion 126

Analyzing – Mastering The Science 140

Planogram Analysis - The Single Planogram 140

Planogram Analysis - The Planogram Project 150

Space Productivity – Macro Space Optimization 158

Execution & Compliance – Mastering The Operations 176

Preparing the Change 178

Making the Change 183

Monitoring & Maintaining the Change 186

How to improve planogram compliance 191

Space Planning Teams - Mastering The Organization 195

The Space Team in Consumer Brands 195

The Space Team in Retailers 199

Where Does Analytics Belong? 204

A Space Planner's Career Path 207

Winners Keep Score 211

Soft Skills - Mastering The Relationships 216

Applying Soft Skills: A day in the life 218

Network your Way to Career Success 225

Appendix 232

What every space planner should know: 232

Off Cycle Planogram Change Pro Forma Template - Blank   234
Off Cycle Planogram Change Pro Forma Template –
filled out   235
Sample Systems Interface Diagram   236
A Sample of Merchandising Guidelines   237
Recommended by the Author   242
About the Author   244

Publisher's Cataloging-in-Publication Data

Names: Delaney, Flora author.

Title: Mastering Retail Space Planning / by Flora Delaney.

Description: Building expertise in retail store space planning, Waterford and Howell Publishing, 2024.

Identifiers: ISBN 979-8-9912261-2-7

Subjects: LCSH Retail trade. | Stores, Retail. | Success in business. | Small business—Management. | Small business marketing. | Marketing—Management. | Shopper services—Management. | Merchandising. | Pricing. | BISAC BUSINESS & ECONOMICS / Sales & Selling / General | BUSINESS & ECONOMICS / Industries / Retailing

Classification: LCC HF5429 .D355 2019 | DDC 658.8/7—dc23

MASTERING RETAIL SPACE PLANNING

This publication is designed to provide accurate and authoritative information in regard to the subject matter covered. It is sold with the understanding that neither the authors not the publisher is engaged in rendering legal, investment, accounting or other professional services. While the publisher and authors have used their best efforts in preparing this book, they make no representations or warranties with respect to the accuracy or completeness of the contents of the book and specifically disclaim any implied warranties or merchantability or fitness for a particular purpose. The advice and strategies contained herein may not be suitable for your situation. You should consult with a professional when appropriate. Neither the publisher nor the authors shall be liable for any loss of profit or any other commercial damages, including but not limited to special, incidental, consequential. Personal or other damages.

For information contact:
https://www.floradelaney.com/contact

Cover design by Michael Rehder
ISBN: 979-8-9912261-2-7

First Edition: September 2024

10 9 8 7 6 5 4 3 2 1

Dedication

To the next generation of retail space planners
who will build the retail emporiums of the future.

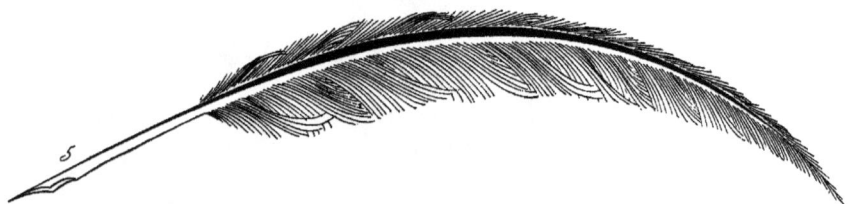

Why Read This Book

This book is meant to accelerate your knowledge of retail space planning. Ideally, it helps people build a retail space planning career. Consider it a guidebook for both the person who is early in their career as a retail space planner as well as a guide for more experienced practitioners. As you read it, consider how you might apply more mastery to your retail space planning career to deliver reliable results for your organization.

This book is for you if:

- You lead a space planning team.
- The leader of a space planning team reports to you.
- You need more insight into how great space planning teams operate.
- You are building a career in space planning and want to build skills in your field.
- You are a new transfer into a space planning team, and you want to gain credibility and insight into your practice.
- You are a supplier, broker or category captain for a retail space planning team.
- You are a technology product manager or someone who must support space planning professionals as part of your job.
- You are a category manager who relies on space planning teams to translate and execute the in-store merchandising directions for your category.
- You are a store team member who wants to understand more about how merchandising changes that affect your store are created.

- You are a process manager that works with either the category or space management functions with a goal to better understand their relationships.
- You are a supply chain team member, and you want to understand how space planning supports with your goals.

The Power of Space Planning

Ask what makes a powerful retail experience and shoppers usually say great customer service, a fun place to shop and great prices. Ask a retailer, and you'll hear about a lean supply chain and efficient store operations. For brands, it's all about customer solutions and product showcasing. In every case, the efforts of everyone to deliver a satisfying experience happens at the shelf. A lot must come together to deliver that memorable retail shopping experience. Category Managers must select the right items. Store operators need to keep a clean shop. Inventory must be in stock. Marketing events need to entice both new customers and lapsed customers. But in the end, it is the planogram – how products are merchandised and showcased at the shelf – that ultimately matters. It affects every item in every store, every customer, every employee, every day. Properly done, a planogram helps the store run more efficiently and delights shoppers. That is the power of space planning.

If you're inclined to think about retail stores as a node in a product's supply chain, then the planogram represents the final four feet of the supply chain. If you think of retail as a marketing space to sell more goods, then the planogram is the final moment that matters in your marketing plans. If you work in a store, then the planogram is your best silent sales partner, helping your customers find and select their best choices from amongst the products in your store. It's no wonder that billion-dollar brands spend incredible resources to influence planogram merchandising: It is where the final sale happens.

Even in the world of e-commerce and shopping from home, there is optimism for what stores of the future will be. Our children may view shopping differently, but there will always be a need for people to go out to the store – to see new things, spend time with other people in a low-key activity and get out of the house. Stores will continue to be the way in which a retail brand comes to life for shoppers. I love the Williams-Sonoma website as much as the next person, but there is nothing like touching gleaming copper pans, feeling the heft of table linens or smelling lemon poppy seed muffins baked in their store. Williams-Sonoma knows that. They know that shoppers conjure up that environment when they scroll the site or get a promotional email.

Because great retailing and great space management are the same. Both the enormous retailing industry and the specific planogramming activity are focused on how a customer encounters products for sale, considers their purchase and makes their selection. Great retailing and great space management make decisions easy for the shopper. The presentation gives them confidence that there is a selection that will meet their needs. Pricing is easy to read and compare. There are acceptable choices for every consideration. Shoppers feel empowered to make good choices for themselves. And all of that happens at the shelf without talking to anyone. Think of it as letting our shelves do the talking.

And by shelves, we mean far more than the regiments of aisles in a store. Space planning includes the entire variety of merchandising elements at a retailer's disposal. Space planning includes the freezer cases, jewelry counters, mannequins atop displays, bookcases, hanging racks, produce tables, working demonstration displays – even outdoor sidewalk space.

When the store experience is inviting, intriguing and well-merchandised, customers buy more than they planned at the onset of their shopping trip. Brilliantly demonstrated by any shopper at an IKEA who intended to buy a bookcase and walked out with candles, a houseplant and wine glasses. It is not a diabolical plan for retailers to pump up margins with extraneous sales. It is an effort to understand shoppers needs so well that when they come in to solve a problem or fill a void, retailers have anticipated their other unmet needs as well. Consider every cross-merchandised placement of batteries near toys, household cleaners near mops or fertilizer with grass seed as perfect examples. Savvy retailers know that shoppers are pressured for time, and they need to be efficient and frugal. Great space planning helps do some of the thinking for them. And if that leads to a bigger transaction, the retailer wins.

There has been merchandising and direction about where to place items in stores for centuries.[1] Computerized space planning was developed in the late twentieth century. One of the first benefits of computerized planograms was visibility to the entire supply chain. Planograms inform inventory systems of the holding capacity at the shelf and can help balance customer demand with store supply levels. For all retailers, product should flow as quickly as possible from the receiving dock to the sales floor. After all, product doesn't sell in the back room. So, planograms are key to ensuring that the flow of goods is as efficient as possible. Pushing back into the supply chain, planogram shelf capacity and unit sales forecasts can help distribution centers calculate the optimal fill rate for each truck to deliver in full cases and optimize DC throughput. This is critically important to delivering in full truckloads to optimize the "sales per gallon" and save on transportation costs.

For retail store associates, the planogram can make the entire store easier to operate. When properly balanced, the shelves provide sufficient inventory to meet customers' demand without out of stocks disappointing them. Product that is received in the back fits entirely on the shelf without the need for

---

[1]　For more see *Retail: The Second-Oldest Profession,* 2019 by the author

upstock[2] or backstock that has to be continually "farmed" to the shelves through the week or day. When new items arrive, the planogram should direct precisely where the new items should be merchandised to make it easy for excited new shoppers to find.

For consumer brands, the planogram is an attractive way to showcase each item within its proper competitive set. Ideally, a planogram makes it evident if the products are valued because of their attractive price, unique flavors, reliability or trendy position. The work that goes into a brand's unique positioning should be apparent by the placement on the planogram. A well-merchandised planogram reinforces the product's attributes and make it easy for shoppers to recognize and select it.

As a financial operation, planograms can drive key metrics that directly impact retail profits. The days of supply on the shelf drive inventory turns (also called turnover) and the return on millions of dollars in inventory investment across a retail chain. Optimally allocated store space drives sales per square foot which is evaluated by store managers and Wall Street alike. Space Planning store layouts can produce "heat maps" to compare the sales performance across the store and bring financial reports to life.

As you will see in this book, space planning is a critical for creating an attractive and profitable retail store. However, we are going to separate it from several other key store design elements that are necessary for creating a powerful branded experience. While store planners *may* be involved with store design, we will not be addressing the architectural elements of a store. The finishes, flooring, lighting and palette which certainly impacts

---

[2] *Upstock* is a common term that retailers use to refer to excess inventory that is placed above a section in a store on an unshoppable shelf. Store operators access that inventory with ladders or scissor lifts and then merchandise it into its home location below on a regular basis. This can help alleviate overcrowding the backroom with excess stock. But it is generally frowned upon due to the excessive labor to place it, track it and then merchandise it again. It is a sign of a retailer with a suboptimized inventory and replenishment practice.

the environment is out of scope. As is the exterior. We will presume that operational considerations like the number of check lanes, vestibule space, and the size of the backroom warehouse are already determined before store layout begins. We are focused on merchandising product within the environment and maximizing its impact no matter what "shell" the store building provides.

Space Planning Power in Action

Let's take a deeper look at examples where highly functioning retailers and brands use space planning to deliver more value to customers and stakeholders. (And drive more sales!)

Our first example is a national retailer who has its own distribution centers across the country. Each DC serves a specific set of stores. The DCs use a warehouse management system (WMS) that builds orders for each store and truck delivery route. It uses a central inventory replenishment system. The WMS is updated with each store's active planogram and floor plan information each night so that it is aware of the aisle and section location for every item in each store.

As it builds the truck order and each case is selected and sorted to be placed on a delivery truck, each carton is tagged with the exact aisle and section location where it should be merchandised within the store receiving the delivery. So, a case of cake mix is labeled "aisle 7, section 4" for one store and "aisle 12, section 5" in a different store. When possible, entire aisles are packed together on half-pallets so that the forklift that removes the pallet from the truck can drive it directly onto the sales floor to its exact aisle location. This simple application of "space awareness" creates efficiency that improves performance both in the DC's and the stores. Products flow over 12 times faster onto the shelves than before.

The second example is one of the most common applications for planogram-ming data. Printing shelf tags in the exact order for the products in the planogram saves store labor and printing costs. Many retailers integrate price changes with planogram data to ensure that pricing labels are specifically printed for each store by aisle, by shelf so that store associates can quickly make all price changes with a single aisle pass through.

Taken even further, a national dollar store chain uses the planogram position data and each product's dimensions to print 4' shelf channel strips with product images, pricing and placement so that store associates can replace the entire shelf strip and simply place items above their pictures to make instant planogram and pricing changes at once. This is especially helpful when a portion of the store associates do not read well or do not use English as their first language.

Finally, more progressive retailers use electronic shelf labels (ESLs) and planograms to monitor and direct all product positions on the shelf. Planogram data combines with pricing data to broadcast pricing changes in real time to the correct ESL in the stores via an internal network. This eliminates printing and store labor costs! (But, of course, there is the initial sunk investment into the cost of the ESLs and their technology.)

Figure 1 : Example of an electronic shelf label

Planograms are also key for store managers and schedule builders to properly plan and budget for merchandising changes in the store. From weekly or monthly promotional end caps to full-on store resets, retailers who use planograms can accurately forecast the amount of time it will take store personnel to make merchandising changes. This is a critical input for building schedules or budgeting for third-party merchandising labor needed at each store. By knowing the time, cost of labor and financial impact of a merchandising change, retailers can control the scope of change to match their available resources. Or, if the sales benefit is great enough, they can budget for additional hours or resources. In any case, it provides management with a reliable estimate that they can use to hold themselves accountable for people in the store.

It is with labor estimates like this that retailers can make an informed decision about the timing for rolling out a new item. When consumer packaged goods companies (CPGs) introduce new items to the market, they usually coordinate with advertising, consumer promotions and other investments. Unfortunately, those introductions do not always coincide with a specific retailer's timing for making merchandising changes. When CPGs want a new item introduced "off cycle," a retailer can use their planogram and labor reset estimates to evaluate if the new product will produce enough sales to justify the labor investment for the unscheduled change. If not, the retailer may ask the CPG to underwrite that unbudgeted cost.

A big box home improvement retailer leveraged their space planning data to create a more efficient returns process. It isn't unusual for do-it-yourselfers to overestimate the materials they need for a project and then return products to the store. The retailer combined space location data with the POS returns protocol to immediately indicate where the "home location" of the returned products belonged. The service counter personnel then sort all returns to their proper cart and indicate exactly where each item should be remerchandised so that returns flow quickly and accurately back onto the sales floor. It makes the process faster and improves inventory turnover because products are not mislocated or left stranded at the returns desk.

Brands that create everything from spray paint to cereal to diapers have a deep interest in making sure they are getting their "fair share" of the shelf to represent their importance to shoppers. Recognizing the need for agility, speed to market and accuracy, many CPGs take on a "category captain" role to help retailers analyze and merchandise category trends. A large portion of the investment is planogram creation and production. For CPGs who recognize that all of their product innovation, marketing and production may fail if a retailer does not execute merchandising well, it is worth hiring resources to make sure that planogram assortments and merchandising meet the highest standards.

Retail financial analysts are constantly searching for ways to extract more productivity from their stores. Why wouldn't they? For most retailers, store leases and locations are the second largest capital expense for their entire company behind inventory. So naturally, retail CFOs have a focus on driving more sales and profit out of every location.

Mature retailers persistently test and evaluate merchandising in stores. They want to determine which positions and adjacencies deliver the best performance. Which departments are leading and lagging in sales per square foot and how to make adjustments that customers will reward with more sales? When products are on promotion, how can they be merchandised in the best location to highlight their value and sell through at their proper time without disappointing shoppers? Should the chain consider a store within a store concept? A placement contract from a key vendor? Or even opening a new banner or store concept? Space panning data and space planning systems provide the means to forecast, test and evaluate all of these scenarios that could lead to millions of dollars in incremental sales or shuttering stores.

A Look Ahead

All of these old school benefits are not the only advantages to be gained through a highly functioning space planning system. Retailers who have an accurate, complete space planning system and data are well positioned for the future as well.

In-store order pickers who select the products from shoppers' online orders are a prime audience. Retailers with a complete store merchandising system (store-specific floorplans and corresponding planograms) can arrange customer orders from the website in aisle order for a particular store and deliver those orders to a phone or other mobile device. So, while the shoppers may see their selections in one hierarchy (for example, they may order eggs, bacon, bananas and oatmeal from the "breakfast section" of the website,) the order pickers will have the entire order arranged to align to their location in the store. Order pickers can even have separate orders threaded through their device so they can compile multiple orders at once. It sets up order selection to be as efficient as possible.

This same access and visibility are just as important to busy shoppers. Using the same data and providing it in a customer-facing app means that shoppers can get even more value using the store's app. Add in real-time inventory and *boom* you have a loyal shopper! Walmart recently highlighted this ability in their app during a holiday advertising campaign recognizing how valuable shopper time is during the busiest time of the year. Just think: You can be a better partner to your shoppers by giving them the information that they need. They will give your company valuable insight into what they want and how they shop. You can create a better store that keeps them happy and engaged by using the data they willingly share.

As retail moves to the metaverse and virtual reality (VR) makes inroads into retailing, shoppers still need to be tethered to the shopping reality they know. Floor plans and planograms are the basis for re-creating a VR store environment where shoppers can interact with products and stores in a familiar manner. There are so many ways that this can benefit retailers:

1. Testing: VR can simulate new stores, remerchandised aisles and in-store marketing campaigns so that retailers can test their impact on shoppers without the expensive step of creating real-world prototypes. It's a great way to extend a retail innovation budget. Plus, because nothing is really "in the market," plans can be kept out of the public eye – and off of the competition's radar. This is particularly critical when there are package changes or pricing changes in test.

2. New markets: VR can open the door to shoppers that a retail brand covets but does not yet have. Whether it's college students, foreign citizens or vacationers, a VR simulation can reach difficult-to-access prospective shoppers anywhere on the globe. Compared to past shopper intercept sites, VR is faster and less expensive to execute.

3. Journey Maps: VR can capture each step in a shopper's journey. Retailers can evaluate how shoppers scan shelves to find products to identify planogram hot spots. Shoppers can "pick up" products and read labels, compare products and prices so that retailers can get insight into how shoppers make their selections. It is an easy way to actively listen to customers and learn from them to make stores better.

Retailers and brands can come together in new ways in the metaverse to conduct virtual test marketing, new product planning and simulated walk-throughs. The promise of virtual reality and space planning is the opportunity for retailers and their partners to collaborate more strategically than ever before. Together, they can jointly make decisions that will be more effective and affordable than either could do separately in the past.

Figure 2: VR image provided by ReadySet® – a VR Space Solution

Virtual reality doesn't end there. Retailers are also experimenting with using VR to create planograms. A planogrammer using a headset can see financial performance and merchandising at the same time. With real-time feedback, the VR session can produce planograms without the need for deep experience in using a planogramming tool. With a headset and gloves anyone can create store design and merchandising that look exactly as it will in stores. What that could mean for space planning is democratizing the space planning process. If "anyone" can put on a headset, glasses or gloves and reorganize the merchandising plan, then everyone can have access to systems that are administered by only a small group today.

Finally, while this entire book will be helpful for anyone in the space planning realm, it is still uncertain how AI will disrupt space planning practices. There are already generative AI-driven applications that are meant to build merchandising solutions in assortment, pricing and promotions. Innovators imagine a time when users can ask an AI to "build a compelling yogurt assortment of two hundred items that would meet the needs of a store in Ventura County, California" which would make a recommended selection. Other innovators see entering a complete history of past promotions as well as submitted vendor offers to a system where an AI could cull the choices to the most effective for a particular holiday or promotional event.

Before we reach that level, AI is being used already in building exception-based flags for retailers looking to understand store conditions. In one example, store teams execute planogram changes and then submit a photo as proof of execution. All the photos are reviewed by an AI engine that compares the photos to the expected planogram and rates each store for their level of compliance. Certainly, image recognition and photo resolution can become blockers, but it is an efficient way to flag those small percentage of stores that have issues for follow up with their District or Region manager.

An exciting deployment for AI is to connect it to the consumer decision trees and the products that represent all of the various nodes on those decision trees. With that insight along with merchandising rules and guidelines, an AI can generate dozens of possible planogram layouts for category managers and space planners to consider. In most retail merchandising, planogram design is usually unchallenged. The overall layout and placement are updated from year to year without the much radical redesign. Sometimes the reason for that is to minimize the effort in the store to update the merchandising at the shelf with new items. But, honestly, sometimes the reason is a lack of time or imagination on the part of the category manager and space planner. Under tight deadlines, the most they can do is swap items on and off the shelves, leaving the overall merchandising layout the same. AI can create and suggest dozens of geometric reconfigurations of a planogram's presentation giving the merchandising team a chance to consider many different ways to present their selection to shoppers. AI can also refine and improve merchandising presentations so that each item's particular goal (inventory availability, support for multi-unit purchases, cross-merchandising with selected items, for example) can be optimized with each successive planogram update.

Will these trends impact your career in Space Planning? I see no reason why not. There could come a time where the example above is amended to: "build a compelling yogurt assortment of two hundred items that would meet the needs of a store in Ventura County, California and organize them in the most efficient configuration to fit into a four-door refrigerated set." With access to the fixture and packaging dimensions and the retailer's merchandising and inventory guidelines, an AI could create a number of different options for possible planograms. While human beings may still be required to validate and nudge the set into a final condition, there is no reason to think that this work could not be outsourced to an AI that could do 90-59% of the work of creating a planogram.

For Floor Planning, applying advanced solutions is more complex. And, if I am honest, the jet fuel for merchandising investments has always come from the deep pockets of consumer packaged goods companies who fund solutions in an attempt to gain a bigger share of the shelf. Floor Planning is almost exclusively a problem that retailers must solve. The lean margins in retail have traditionally meant that solution providers could not justify developing expensive solutions because retailers were not a rich enough market to warrant the necessary payback. So, an AI solution in floor planning is likely to be further in the future than for planogramming. I have seen such a solution, and it will be in the US market shortly.

Nevertheless, the VR solutions for 3D store renderings and experimentation could be a viable future solution. Especially given the millions of dollars that retailers invest in putting new store prototypes into the market.

So, there are many ways to consider the advances of space planning in the future. Will there be even more integrations to store operations? Will automation leapfrog current production obstacles with AI? Perhaps. But it will all start with industry leaders who have the vision and mastery over space planning. I hope this book helps you on your journey.

Floor Planning - Mastering The Design

E ach store is unique. Even if it shares the exact layout and fixtures as another store, its sales rates and shopper base will make it unique. So, every single store must have its own floorplan or store map to contain all of the information that a space planning system can know about a store. In many ways, the floor plan is the critical foundation upon which all other merchandising functions depend. It is why this book begins with the floor planning. Everything comes from the floor plan and then ties back to the store's floor plan. So having accurate floor plans is key to a sound space planning practice.

Floor plans are not static. Or, at least, they shouldn't be. Businesses within the store are dynamic. They increase and decrease over time. Customers age. Product offerings change. Trends and technology create demand. Over time, the space allocation inside stores should change too so that the stores adjust to the changes and continue to meet shopper expectations.

Floorplans and the macro use of store space are tightly aligned to a store's brand promise. If a store's strategic brand statement is to carry fresh, local seafood then it should have a statement in either where seafood is located in its stores or how much space is allocated to seafood – or both. A fashion retailer will place its latest collection at the entry because it promises to carry the latest styles. Thus, floor plans and strategic planning should be in constant calibration to ensure that stores are up to date and accurate.

The Blueprint versus The Floorplan

Let's be clear about the difference between a blueprint for a store and a floorplan.

A blueprint for a store is used by the construction teams and contains the technical drawing and representation for all of the elements of the structure of the building. Some of those elements are also foundational for floorplans. While others are not.

The floorplan for a store maps the location for every business or category that a shopper will encounter while navigating the store. The floorplan dictates the location, space allocation and adjacencies for business lines that the store is intended to sell. These merchandising plans change over time to account for the dynamic changes in customer demand as well as the strategic plans that a retailer determines is best for their profitability.

The Elements of a Store Blueprint

	Used by Floor Planning	Not Used by Floor Planning
Title Block:		
• Store Project Name	✓	
• Architect name/firm		✓
• Location	✓	
• Scale of drawing	✓	
• Date of issue	✓	
Site Plan:		
• Property Overview		✓
• Access Points/Driveways		✓
• Landscaping Elements		✓
• Exterior utility lines		✓
Elevations:		
• Exterior Perspectives		✓
• Entrance Appearance		✓
• Heights of exterior elements		✓
• Material Indications		✓
Floor Plans:		
• Interior dimensions	✓	
• Locations of doors & windows	✓	
• Walls, Partitions & Openings	✓	
• Dock and access to public corridors	✓	
• Stairs, Elevators	✓	
• Support Columns	✓	
• Cash Lanes	✓	
Mechanicals:		
• HVAC Layout		✓
• Electrical Wiring diagrams		✓
• Plumbing and Drainage		✓
• Lighting plan		✓
Roof Plan:		
• Roof Layout		✓
• Roofing Materials		✓
• Roof Openings, Access, Vents		✓

There are other elements that may also be included in the set of prints for a store. The foundation plan, computer cabling and access points, enlarged details and details about doors and windows can also be included. But as you can see, it is really the elements in the floorplan layer that will be important to a space planning team.

It isn't unusual to have a store designing team that sits between the architects and the merchandise planners who work within a space planning team to make the store's merchandising floor plan. The store designers usually direct the expensive store capital elements that must be placed before the store can be merchandised. Those elements can include the exact placement for cash registers, walk in coolers and freezers, food preparation stations, shopper accessible freezers and coolers, cameras and loss prevention stanchions, cart corrals and more. Think of them as the permanent furnishings within a store that will not be easily changed over the years.

They make decisions and placements based on the company's strategic store prototype as swell as location-specific forecasts. For example, the number of check lanes that a store will require is in direct relation to the number of customers it expects to serve in the years to come. A site forecast before a store opens helps store designers anticipate the average, and the highest volume peaks a store might expect. Backroom operations will help determine if a store requires extra receiving docks, a secured lockup area for valuable stock or parking for forklifts or other equipment. Local and state regulations can stipulate restroom requirements, store employee accommodations and emergency escape routes. All of those decisions and placements may happen before the floor planners begin to map out where businesses will be located in the store.

The Layers of a Floor Plan

As the floor layout process begins, the floor planner will usually start with a prototype or a block plan for the store. Block plans are like guides that guide the overall placement of key departments and features in the store. It is a reference for placement but not necessarily a strict directive. Floor planners will use the block plan for general guidance but customize the layout for each specific store's condition.

An architect and store designer typically work in AutoCAD® to create the store's plans up to this point. AutoCAD® is a software package from Autodesk®, but it is also the short-hand term that nearly all designers use for a host of designing and planning solutions including Dassault's Solidworks® and Autodesk's Revit®. They are all planning and designing tools that ultimately create the blueprints for a site. AutoCAD's® file type is universally read by construction teams and is the typical submission for inspections and approvals before construction begins.

AutoCAD® uses a system of layers to organize all the objects that a user needs to design a store. Users can click on/off the various layers if they wish to see the store design with or without the lighting plan or plumbing plan, for example. The concept of "layers" reduces the visual clutter by hiding or revealing the elements that a user needs at any given time. That concept of "layers" was adapted by merchandising floor planning tool and is a useful way to conceptualize both the physical elements and the data elements contained in a floor plan.

Within AutoCAD®, there are different ways to represent and populate the geometric shapes that make up a floor plan. At the simplest level, the rectangles and other shapes on the floor plan represent the aisle ways and fixtures that sit on the sales floor. These "regular blocks" are nothing more than the shapes themselves. They have no more data or intelligence than if you were to use a stencil and trace a shape onto a piece of paper. That is why most retailers use "dynamic blocks" in AutoCAD® which are data-driven blocks that can contain data which can be queried and changed using standard database tools.

Most people use dynamic blocks to improve their efficiency by setting up controls, sizes and constraints for typical store furnishings so that they can quickly place "runs" of fixtures that snap together and can be stretched or moved quickly. But advanced users also leverage the attribute definitions that can be tied to an AutoCAD® block so that they can get richer data in their floorplans. Attributes can store things like the fixture component part names and numbers. But also, it can store planogram assignments and annual sales or other performance data. For clever AutoCAD® users, integrations between planogramming, performance data in a data warehouse and fixture ordering information can be consolidated in AutoCAD® files and its data structure. AutoLISP® scripts can automate fetching and populating the floorplans with updated information.

But first, let's begin by talking about a simple approach to the "layers" of a store floor plan that correlate to physical elements. The store has runs of gondolas or islands of displays and rounders that are physically set up on the floor of the store. Those areas of the store typically have unseen boundaries that designate departments. In a grocery store, there is the produce department, the meat and seafood department, the center store (dry goods), and the frozen departments. Those boundaries are larger than any single fixture. So, the floorplan would have the floor, then atop it the department boundary, then the fixtures sit within the departments and finally categories are applied to the fixtures. Thus, the health and beauty aids department might have long runs of shelving where eight feet of oral care sits beside sixteen feet of haircare which is adjacent to four feet of deodorant or shaving. Also, within that department, oval outposts of cosmetics and nailcare add a bit of trendy fashion to an otherwise functional business. Those business lines ought to directly correspond to a planogram where the eight feet of oral care on a floor plan is directly linked to the exact assortment that store should receive of toothpaste and mouthwash and the planogram directs exactly how those items should be presented to shoppers.

This linking of a planogram to a fixture on a floorplan (which belongs to a specific store) is called the "planogram assignment." Planogram assignments are the key link to ensure that the eight layers listed below are aligned and accurate. The planogram assignment is what creates the rich data that downstream price tag systems, supply chain systems, allocation and replenishment systems require from a robust space planning system.

The layers are:

1. Chains (banners) contain regions
2. Regions contain districts
3. Districts contain stores — this hierarchy of stores can proliferate into zones, markets, etc.
4. Stores contain floors
5. Floors contain departments
6. Departments contain fixtures
7. Fixtures contain planograms
8. Planograms contain items

All of these things can change. But the cost of changing them and how it gets done requires different protocols and systems.

Chains regularly reorganize their stores into and out of markets, zones, districts and regions. These "re-orgs" are usually combined with headcount and management changes. But when it happens, systems must reflect both the change and the date the change occurred to keep current and historical reporting accurate.

Infrequently, store remodels will change department sizes and locations along with the physical shelving within a store. Most retailers record them as "major" remodels because the cost of the remodel and fixturing is a capital expenditure that changes the balance sheet (investment) for the store itself.

Contrast that with merchandising changes were business lines are expanded, reduced or moved and adjacencies are reflowed across the shelves as they currently exist. Those efforts do not impact the balance sheet. But the labor, signs and inventory changes impact the P&L as expenses in financial reporting.

Sometimes an illustration helps:

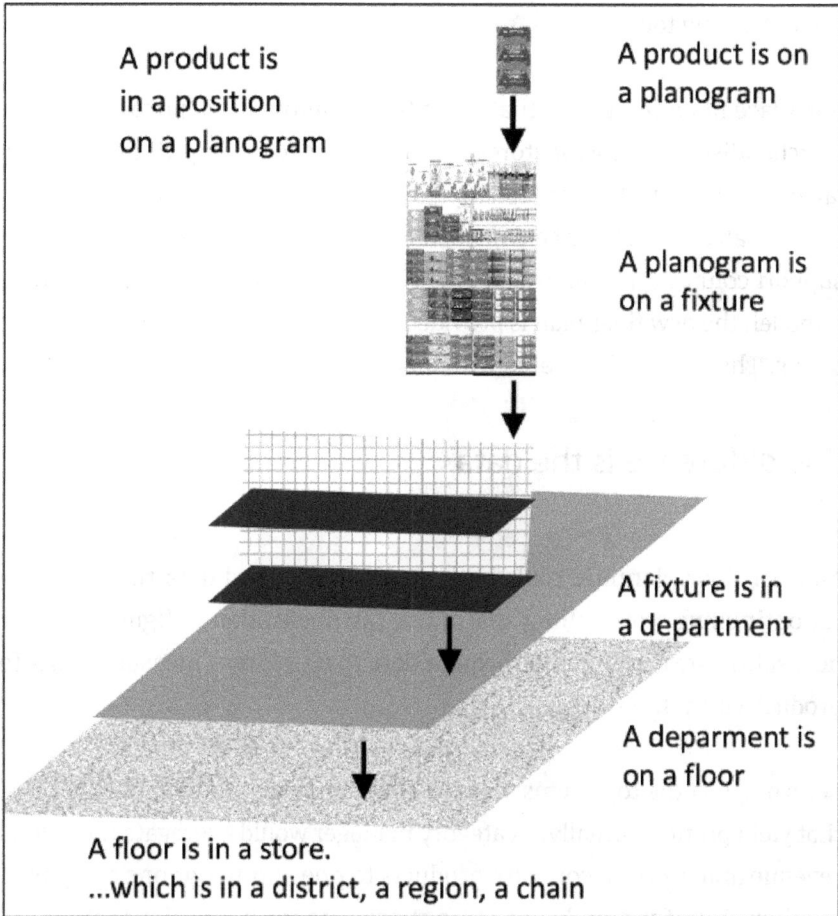

A product is
in a position
on a planogram

A product is on
a planogram

A planogram is
on a fixture

A fixture is in
a department

A deparment is
on a floor

A floor is in a store.
...which is in a district, a region, a chain

Figure 3: A visual model for the layers for space planning.[3]

---

[3] Note that a product is actually in one (or more) *Positions* on the planogram. Which is another conceptual layer to consider in Space Planning but not relevant to Macro Space Planning.

For the floor planner, AutoCAD® can be leveraged to contain all of these "layers" but it is not purpose built for the kinds of analysis and optimization that a true merchandise floor planning application can do. If a space planning team chooses to use AutoCAD® for its merchandise planning for each store, it will have to invest a significant effort to create the data reporting and analytics outside of AutoCAD® that would natively exist in a merchandising floor planning tool.

For space planning teams that use a floor planning tool purpose built for merchandise planning for stores, they will need to begin with the floor plan layer of the AutoCAD® file. Usually this is done as a one-time extract which includes all of the relevant elements that a floor planner needs like entrances, support columns, power drops, etc. Whenever the store undergoes a major remodel, the new floor plan is provided by the construction and store design teams. Then it can be updated with its new merchandising plan.

The difference is the data

Modern floor planning tools both create and record data that is critical for optimizing store selling space. Use the illustration in figure 3 to track how sales data combines with space data to create new measurements for productivity at the store level.

Let's begin at the top. Items are sold at various rates and a variety of prices that yield profit. Normally, a category manager would aggregate the volume, revenue and profit to compare products to one another or one category to another. But if we apply the store space lens to those sales metrics. we can use a floorplanning tool to evaluate the productivity of one section of a single planogram to another. We can compare sales per square feet for one planogram in an aisle to every other planogram in that aisle. A space planner could decide to aware or surrender space to that category to improve the overall sales production on that aisle. Taking that a step further, the sales for all of the space for a department can be compared to other departments to make macros space decisions.

The basic space productivity metric is always:

$$\frac{The\ Performance\ Metric}{The\ Space\ Metric}$$

Thus, department annual sales per square foot is:

$$\frac{Total\ \$\ Department\ Revenue\ for\ 52\ weeks}{Length\ X\ Depth\ of\ the\ Department\ on\ the\ floorplan}$$

Or category profit contribution per linear foot is:

$$\frac{Total\ Category\ Net\ Profit\ \$\ over\ 52\ weeks}{Length\ of\ the\ category\ on\ the\ floorplan}$$

If a floor planning tool is not ingesting or accessing sales data, the metrics must be calculated outside the space planning tool. Many enterprises prefer to use an advanced data analytics platform to provide access to these metrics outside the space planning user group. If so, the floor planning team must regularly reflect all floor plan changes in their data export to the enterprise data aggregator. Ideally, that is a simple API to the floor planning database. Otherwise, there may need to be manual floorplan measurements that are exported to the analytics location.

And there lies the problem. The problem is always the denominator. That bottom part of the calculation. It isn't that hard to aggregate the sales of an item. Whether it comes from its home location or a secondary display, the UPC will control and measure that sale properly. But space can be a much more difficult thing to measure.

The Problems with the Space Denominator

In nearly every situation, measuring store space will be challenged by all or some of the following common situations. As an advisor, there are a few ways that I can help a space planner address these issues. But perhaps the most important thing is to select an approach, document it and be consistent in how it is applied in every store for every category. People of high integrity and deep convictions will have differences of opinions about how to resolve these space denominator problems. That means it is critical that an organization agree on one single approach to solve each of these challenges and stick with it. Inconsistencies where some departments are measured one way while others are measured differently may seem reasonable when viewed from a particular framework. But ultimately, chainwide comparison overtime will be compromised if there isn't a disciplined approach to measuring space.

First, a very common problem is that the merchandising hierarchy (how the category is financially organized) is not the same as the way that category is merchandised in the store. For example, the merchandise hierarchy for the category "haircare" may include the subcategories "shampoo", "conditioner" and "styling aids."

Some stores may have a very large contiguous section that they call "haircare" and let's say a thirty-two-foot planogram contains all shampoos and conditioners and styling aids. It will be very easy to create space metrics where the planogram and the category are one for one.

Other stores have a twenty foot "shampoo and conditioner" planogram and a twelve foot "styling aids" planogram across the aisle. Again, not all that difficult to aggregate those planogram space dimensions to create accurate reporting.

But what if a selection of shampoos is not in the haircare area? They are merchandised in the baby area with diapers, wipes and baby bath products. How will we account for those products? Especially since the name of the planogram "baby care" doesn't provide the clue that there will be shampoos in the section? So even though the category manager creates the full assortment for shampoos, including baby shampoos, the space is not easy to identify for each item. Making it super difficult is when the category manager days they want to do a one for one swap and they want to replace a poor performing baby shampoo with an expensive new dandruff shampoo. While the assortment planning tool may see those as a one for one swap, the space made in one planogram will not create a location for the dandruff shampoo in the other planogram. An intelligent space planning tool can help.

A second problem is that space changes over time. Merchandising changes in stores never line up to scheduled fiscal periods. So, when a category manager wants to review their space productivity for the last fiscal year, the space locations and allocations could have changed many times across the stores in the chain.

Let's say a category manager wants to evaluate the space productivity for the condiment category across the chain for the most recent 52 weeks. But during those 52 weeks, the merchandising for condiments changed dramatically:

Halfway through the year, the chain decided to create a new "international" section to pull together related items into one section for shoppers. All German mustards, soy sauces and Asian sauces were moved out of the condiment section into the international section which ranged in size from 12' to 60' depending on store size. The new space was used to expand ketchup and barbecue sauce from May until September. Then the condiment planogram was reset in the fall, reducing barbecue sauce but expanding mayonnaise. In small stores, the change was minimal, but in larger stores, the shift was over twenty linear feet of shelf space. Finally, there was a test in Florida to replace low selling national brands with an emerging new Cuban condiment brand that has a strong local following.

How does an analyst get visibility to all of these changes at the store level and then aggregate them up to the chain? The permutations are too complex to be accounted for in a standard analytics tool. The reporting must account for both a time dimension – because space changed over time – as well as a store-specific dimension because the changes did not happen everywhere at once. An intelligent space planning tool can help.

Third, the overall space allocation in stores changes over time through both promotional and seasonal changes that can distort space productivity measurements.

A common example is the constant volume of carbonated sodas that sell from store vestibule and entryways compared to their home locations. Sparkling water, beer and other case goods that get stacked in outposts can profoundly bias the results of measuring sales to space. Categories like soda will always appear to need more space than their home locations while other categories that rarely get promotional space, like breakfast sausage, will always look like they are underperforming.

Plus, all promotional space is not the same. Very often stores will be directed to place a promotional program on an endcap. Let's say it is graham crackers, marshmallows and chocolate bars for a s'mores sale. Some stores will have the room to place it on a front-facing endcap. Some will only have enough room to put it on a side wing. Sometimes it will share a cookies endcap. Still others will use dump bins in the aisles. How should that be reflected when there is a sales lift for those items? Where did the sales come from? It requires deep process compliance for even the most sophisticated space planning system to accurately record.

This is extreme when you consider stores that have outdoor yards or other spaces that are the natural home locations for some business lines, but only for a part of the year. Retailers must reconcile how to properly compare space productivity for businesses like plants, charcoal grills and lawn mowers when they are sold from the sidewalk or other "outdoor" areas. Especially, in northern climates when that outdoor area is not available nor stocked year-round.

Finally, when measuring space allocations, there must be alignment on what is being measured. Is it limited to the merchandised space within a store? Meaning just the portion of the sales floor that has merchandise above it? Or is there an attempt to reconcile the entire total store footprint to the various businesses and operations that are housed above it? Retailers who are attempting to prorate rent and operational expenses back to business lines to create true profit contributions (P&L's) for the businesses must allocate aisle space and shared spaces back to businesses so that the entire store's selling space is accounted for.

It is generally a best practice to measure department space allocations including aisleways. That practice will capture promotional displays, in-aisle product stacks and non-uniform presentations on pinwheels and rounders accurately for the department. Once the store has been divided into its component departments, measure the truly shared spaces such as the customer service counter, cart corral, cash registers and other operational areas and prorate their space back to the departments on a prorated bases (typically based on percent of sales.)

Departmental space measurements to create the space denominator are not particularly difficult. But taking that a step deeper to category measurements create new challenges. In general, it is a good practice to allocate half of the aisle space in front of a planogram to the back of the backboard for planogrammed categories. This becomes the "area" of the store that is allocated to the planogram. If the planogram houses more than one category, prorate the space to the categories based on percent of sales from that planogram as listed above.

The trouble comes when measuring non-rectangular and non-uniform spaces. Consider a category that faces a major traffic lane in the store where the walkway is double the width of the standard interior aisleways. Is it fair to "punish" that planogram with more space allocation than if it were facing an interior aisle on the other side of the gondola? What about round or curved presentations? Or businesses that wrap around an end and continue on another aisle?

These examples are common and quite often become insurmountable when an organization tries to extend AutoCAD® or another construction design program into merchandising plans for stores. Even with floor planning tools, they are thorny problems to overcome. But at least if an enterprise is using a proper merchandising floorplanning tool with an integrated database, there is a possible way to resolve these common issues.

Otherwise, the power of space measurements remains locked inside tools that were not meant to become the basis for reporting. Executives and retail leaders develop blind spots where they cannot measure the outcome of decisions. Stores grow stale. Merchandising changes are rare, and customers are fickle. They adopt new shopping patterns faster than our stores can keep up. Profits tumble. There's a lot at stake which can be addressed with proper floor planning and space planning tools.

For more on this, turn to Chapter 7: Analyzing: Mastering the Science.

Basic Floor Planning Designs

As a floor planner, you may or may not get to influence the placement of fixtures within a department. If you do, you may find yourself collaborating with procurement who will order the fixtures. Or execution teams who will assemble and place the fixtures. Or department vice presidents who will have opinions about how they want to highlight businesses. You will most certainly interact with the store designers.

Let's take a look at the most common ways to organize store fixtures and store designs.

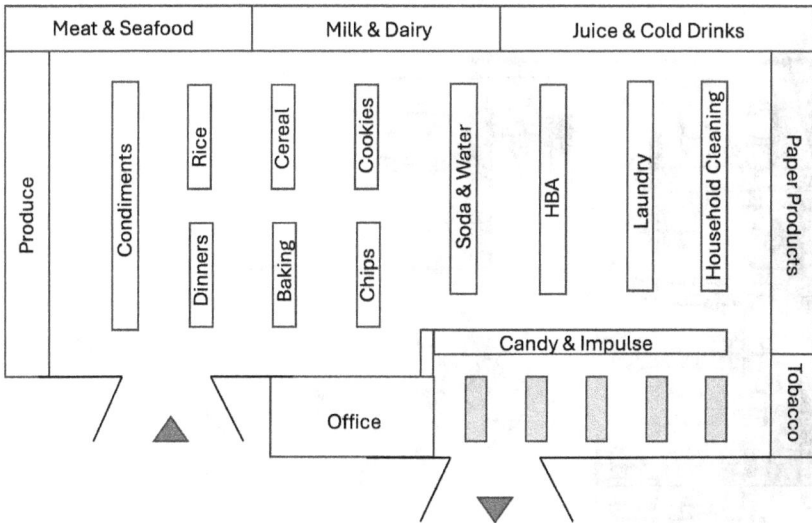

Figure 4: A Grid Design

A grid floor plan features row after row of long aisles. It is designed to maximize every inch of floor space and be efficient to shop in its entirety. Making it great for grocery, big box and hardware stores that have lots of merchandise in a variety of categories. But department interests are usually relegated to perimeters while the center store stolidly remains.

Shoppers are familiar with this layout. Most people find it easy to navigate and understand even if it is the first time they have entered a store. Retailers hope the long aisles encourage browsing past items shoppers didn't plan to buy while on the hunt for the one they want. Consequently, adjacencies are critical. Endcaps in a grid are limited and are prime real estate for promotional items. Both can spur an impulse buy.

On the downside, this isn't a very exciting layout. It can come across as too clean and uninspired. It's great for efficiency, but not aligned for upscale brands, shopping as recreation or the thrill of the hunt.

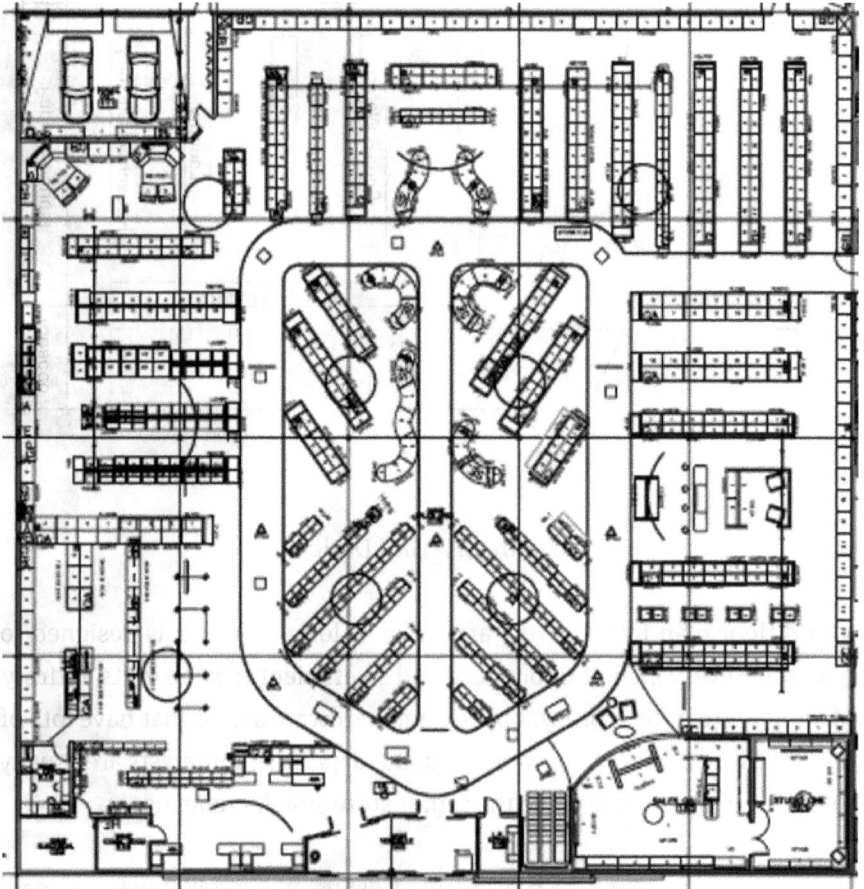

Figure 5: A Racetrack Design

The racetrack layout creates a closed loop that leads customers from the front of the store, past every department, and then to the check-out. Many retailers with this design, use flooring changes (tile, carpet, etc.) to create natural "department" barriers to help shoppers navigate it more easily.

It works well for retail stores where customers are willing to browse rather than focus on an efficient in-and-out shopping trip. To make this store design easier to navigate, consider populating the central area with shorter shelves so that shoppers in the middle of the store can see way finding signs along the perimeter walls. Or, if your intent is to create stores-within-a-store, you can use taller shelves to create visual barriers between shops.

Racetracks, sometimes called loops, are great for making sure every product category or department is visible. This design creates the greatest number of endcaps and display areas throughout the store. Consider this option when you have an operating model that "sells" promotional space to suppliers for key time periods.

This design makes the most out of a limited display area by maximizing perimeter walls. Consider the "shopability" of those tall exterior walls and be sure that you can create a neat and attractive appearance of goods that rise along those walls.

This is also a fine option when a store has multiple entrances.

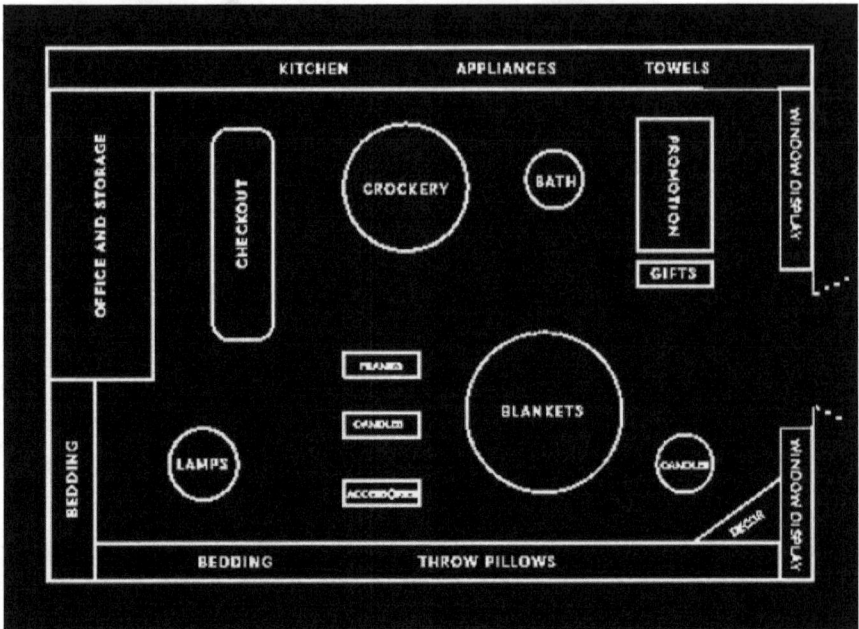

Figure 6 : A Free-Flow Design

A free flow design does not designate a path for shoppers to follow. The point is that the store can be navigated as a shopper chooses. Specialty and boutique stores commonly use this style of store layout. It is executed with freestanding fixtures that are placed at angles and in groupings to encourage shoppers to slow down and explore.

Without any definite traffic flow, the plan counts on creative merchandisers to create eye-catching displays that draw shoppers toward different zones in the store. What makes it so popular is that it can be reconfigured at will. Making it supremely customizable. Perfect for stores that carry a wide array of changing goods. This is especially useful for stores that carry fast changing trendy goods.

This layout works best for a store that has a smaller inventory and necessitates slower browsing. When products are given "space to breathe," it can be a relaxing and interesting destination. But it can quickly feel chaotic and cluttered when fixtures are too close together or overloaded with product. For this reason, to succeed there has to be outstanding merchandising skills amongst the people who work in the store and clear communication to create an inviting store environment.

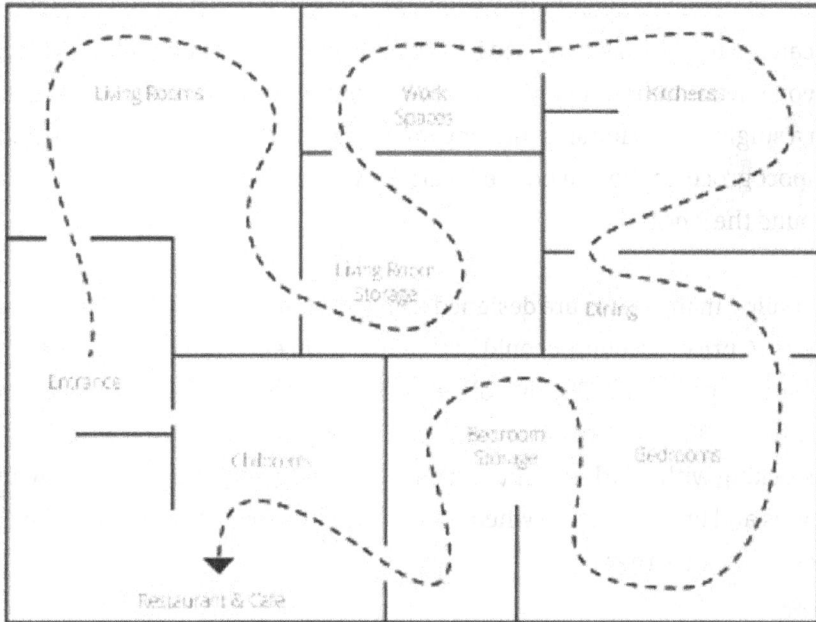

Figure 7: A Directed Path Design

A directed path design creates a highly controlled flow through a store If you have ever been to an IKEA, you have seen this style of store design.

Once shoppers are in the store, there is really only one single path to move from the entrance to the exit. For store designers who want to create a very specific store experience for their shoppers, this is a way to ensure that elements are presented in a specific order. And it creates certainty that the entire store is shopped.

But customers can find this design constricting and feel uncomfortable when they are unable to select their own way through a store. It is the store designer's responsibility when they use this approach to enchant their shoppers with new experiences at each turn. As such, it is a risky design choice unless you have the dedication to pull it off.

It can be successful when used in moderation, however. Consider this style if you have a multi-story store and you want to create a special experience on a single floor. Home furnishing stores can do this well. As can specialty import grocers who can create locations within their store for foods from around the world.

In reality, many stores are designed using a combination of different design styles. A price discounter could have a free form entry way that leads to the apparel department. The overall store is built around a racetrack pathway. But the back half of the store is a grid design to maximize efficiency for restocking with a forklift. But as a tore planner, being able to recognize the deigns and understanding when they should be used will make you a better store design partner.

The Fundamentals of Floor Planning

During the store design process, ultimately you will arrive at a point where fixture placement is resolved and final. Then, it will be your job to place businesses (and, thus, planograms) onto those fixtures. At the most basic level, there are three things you can control:

1. **Absolute Location** – Precisely where in a store will a business be located? Interior/Perimeter? Back/Front? Left/Right/Center? Location in a store is closely tied to branding for the store, each category's strategy and planned traffic flow. For example, a store that built its brand as a

destination for denim jeans for the entire family may decide to place all denim at the back half of the store. Since customers are entering the store specifically to purchase denim, in all likelihood, placing the denim deeper in the store will require shoppers to walk past other categories that may induce them to make an unplanned purchase. If novelty socks have a convenience strategy in the same store's portfolio, placement of those items near check lanes could spur an impulse buy.

2. **Space Allocation** – How large will the footprint be for each business on the sales floor? Space allocation is one floor planning decision where analytics and optimization can help floor planners make sound decisions. Space allocation is usually based on sales rates, strategic sales forecasts, the physical size of the products for sale and their merchandising style. The decision on space allocation will typically control how broad the selection will be for that store and how much inventory a business can place on the sales floor.

3. **Adjacencies** – Which other businesses will surround a category? How can adjacent placements increase a shoppers' overall purchase? Adjacencies can be improved by market basket analyses to understand the relationships between products that are frequently purchased together. What a floor planner can influence is not necessarily the purchasing relationship between two products (the percentage of shoppers who purchase milk and cereal together) but the sales lift for a product. (How much more common is hot cocoa mix is purchased with milk than is purchased without milk.) In this relationship there is usually a core item (the milk) and a supported item (the cocoa mix.) Floor planners are well advised to work with the strategic category management teams to deeply understand shopping occasions and full solution selling campaigns.

As you start to place merchandise categories on the floor plan, there are some business lines that are non-negotiable. Ice cream must go in a freezer case. The fresh seafood counter must have access to the walk-in cooler. As you start to design the store, place those business lines that must be tethered to a specific location. This will start to define your departments. Also, take time to evaluate the natural traffic intersections that will occur in the store and where high volumes of shopper traffic will move. It will be important to consider those locations for impulse categories, promotional and seasonal placements.

Floor planners think about the visual valleys that are created by tall fixtures that block a shopper's view to other parts of the store. Everything in that valley should be related and help a shopper who is at the store for a specific shopping mission. Mission-driven shopping is a category management concept that describes when a shopper needs to fulfill a specific need while shopping. Maybe they are turning an extra bedroom into a nursery. Maybe they are getting dorm supplies for college. Or maybe they are getting food for a weekend barbecue. Floor planners who understand the shopping missions that category managers select their products to fulfill, can make decisions about floor planning placements that reinforce the overall customer experience during those shopping missions.

It is one reason why household cleaning supplies and air fresheners are typically in the same valley. The household cleaning mission solves a problem for shoppers and delivers a final outcome: a clean, fresh-smelling home.

As you think about the departments and valleys in the store design, consider the need to a variety of fixture types and their operational and shopping requirements. If there are departments that have large goods or pallets on the sales floor, aisleways must be wide enough for forklift access and to turn around. Apparel fixtures must include space for two shoppers back-to-back[4]

---

[4] Paco Underhill in "*Why We Buy: The Science of Shopping*", (1999, New York, NY: Simon & Schuster) coined the phrase "butt brush factor" for when store spaces are packed too closely and shoppers in narrow aisles are forced to accidentally brush one another from behind. Customers are uncomfortable and dislike their shopping experience without being able to identify why. Over time, shoppers abandon stores where they dislike shopping. A savvy floor planner considers this in their fixture placement and store design.

to pull hangers off rods. And they must be close to fitting rooms.

Prototypes and Templates

Our stores need to deliver a consistent, reliable shopping experience. Uniformity helps make our stores easier to operate. It is one of the many ways that we deliver a stable brand promise that shoppers can rely on.

For floor planners, understanding a store's prototype will make placement and adjacency planning more consistent. Prototypes usually refer to several things at once. First is the general size and shape of the store design. Second, is the era of the store's opening date. Combined, those elements can usually describe the type of store that someone can expect. For example, a "Prototype 1.0" may describe the first stores that the chain put into the market in the 1990's that were 10,000-15,000 sf, had a single entry in the middle of the storefront, 8-10 checkout lanes, white fixtures and was wider than it was deep. In the 2000's, the chain opened "Prototype 2.0" that were 20,000-24,000 sf, had two entries on each side of the storefront, 12 checkout lanes that shared a customer queue, and a racetrack interior with beige and honey oak fixtures. Thus, prototypes can quickly become shorthand for the style of a store and how it is configured.

Chains have dozens of prototypes - especially if they acquired stores through mergers or acquisitions. And even if every store is a unique property and design, the use of a prototype name to help describe store groups is helpful for a chain of stores. Prototype names themselves can be descriptive: like "two story with rooftop parking", "side entry with secured back lot", "pharmacy right, salon left", "backwall fitting rooms with mall-side entry." As you can see, using a store design prototype can help when communicating store level analyses or planning to make major changes.

Prototyping is useful in project planning for major changes or remerchandising, when a template is developed for each prototype to support the change. Rather than reviewing every store, templates that gets reviewed and approved during the strategic project planning. (Naturally, every store plan must be individually reviewed during execution. But for company executives, reviewing and approving templates is standard.)

Imagine that a major remodel will insert a 4,000 square foot tableware department into a housewares and furnishings store. To make room for such a large department, the space will come from a variety of places depending on each store's performance and prototype. So rather than create a plan from scratch for each store, the space planning team partners with construction and data analytics to build the ideal placement changes by prototype. Those templates then get approved and become the blueprint for all the stores that share that prototype.

Templates can also serve to speed up floor plan execution. Some software provides "cut and paste" functionality so that floor planners can make store floor plan changes very quickly to individual store plans. They can isolate the section of the store that needs to change and apply the "cut and paste" section to the store plan. Usually, there is additional work that needs to be done to ensure the proper fit for each store. But the use of floorplan prototypes and templates can improve a company's communication, approval processes and execution speed.

Influencing Shoppers - Mastering The Psychology

T he best retailers know: It isn't about the products. Or the stores. Or fantastic deals. It is about the shopper. Every single shopper represents someone who needs something. It can be as critical as medicine for a sick infant or as trifling as a new dress for vacation. But each shopper goes into a store with a hope that they will be delighted to find what they need at a price they can afford. Our job as space planners is to make our stores attractive and easy to shop. We want shoppers to find what they are looking for *plus*...a little something extra. "The need and the want." As retailers, our goal is to satisfy both. And our merchandising communicates that. Said another way, great space planners understand the mind of their shoppers.

Stores in the United States are among the largest in the world. Our shoppers have to trek across the parking lot to come inside a 50,000 square foot grocery store. Or even a 200,000 square foot store if it is a big box or warehouse store. Then they must navigate tens of thousands of items to find their selection. At the same time that our stores get larger, the products for sale are more varied. Brands add seasonal items, limited editions, multi-packs and sample sizes. Repackaging and rebranding can confuse shoppers looking for "the usual." On top of that, shoppers are more pressed for time. According to the Time Use Institute, shoppers spend an average of 41 minutes in a grocery store shopping trip – and 8 minutes of that is in the checkout line. Which means a shopper navigates and shops the entire store in 33 minutes. For convenience stores, the shopping trip is under 4 minutes!

All of which means that our stores have be easy to understand to help shoppers quickly evaluate their options and make a choice. Because while they are making their purchases, they are also judging our stores. Are they clean? Are they inviting? Do they enjoy the experience? Or is it time that they try somewhere else? A lot is at stake in the short time they are in our stores.

Shoppers at the Center

So what can a retailer do to become and remain a shopper's top choice?

1. Put the shopper at the center of everything. Retailers need to have a very clear view of their shopper and what they need. It is why Kohls and Nordstroms can operate with many similar departments (women's fashion, footwear, home goods) but still have very different offerings. They each understand who their shopper is and how to cater to them properly.
2. Be Predictable. Shoppers like to rely on a consistent experience when they enter a store. Sure – they want to see new products and be enticed with new offerings. But it has to make sense. Air fresheners in an auto parts store is one thing. Sushi is quite another. It is why shoppers can readily enter a chain store on vacation and navigate it well even if it is a thousand miles away from their home store. They know what to expect from a Walgreens or a Target. There is consistency in terms of the selection they will carry, the price points and the store layout.
3. Satisfy and Delight. Like Maslow's hierarchy of needs, retailers must first satisfy their target shoppers. That means they have to be in stock on the destination products that attract shoppers in the first place. Shoppers have to rely on a consistent level of satisfaction for products,

price and customer service to create loyalty to a store. Then to keep them returning, delight your shoppers. Some stores do that through free product sampling and demonstrations. Others create a "treasure hunt" at the store front to keep customers interested in the latest deals. Whether it is exclusive access to the latest fashions or free gift wrapping, stores that delight shoppers with something unexpected will be rewarded with life long shoppers.

Six Shopping Trips

Just as a retailer should understand its shoppers, we also need to understand the purpose for each shopping trip. Because the same shopper can have a different shopping mission at different times which causes them to behave differently.

For example, and consumer electronics store could focus its target on family men between 25-45 who have a deep penchant for technology. They can deeply research their behavior and understand how they make decisions. Perhaps they know that one of their motivations is that they love to spend time with family streaming action movies to their home cinema. But if it is Christmas and the shopping mission is to buy a gift for his mother, he may suddenly behave differently. Will they anticipate that this same shopper will veer off from the home entertainment center to browse electric tea kettles?

Understanding shopping missions is especially important for floor planners who decide on the location and adjacency of related businesses. Shopping missions can determine how products within stores should be organized and how adjacencies and placement should vary.

Here are the six most common shopping trip types:

Immediate Consumption – shoppers are looking for something they will immediately use or eat. As such, being in stock is non-negotiable. If a shopper wants a Snickers bar, but it is out of stock, then they are nearly always going to select something else rather than go to another store.

- Immediate consumption trips require proper temperature (no warm beer.)
- Immediate consumption may require adjacent utensils or condiments.
- Immediate consumption usually means single-service packaging.

Shopping List Driven – Shoppers are looking for specific items to meet a recipe, project or fill a pantry void. Much can be learned about shopping behavior from looking at a shopping list. Notice the difference in substitutability between a shopper who writes "juice for breakfast" on their list versus "orange juice - no pulp." Shoppers who are using a list may make another choice if their first selection is not available. But they may also change stores. With online orders delivered to their homes, expect less willingness to compromise.

Stock-Up – Shoppers on a stock up mission are looking for deals on consumable items. Not necessarily items they will eat. But items that they will use up and need to replenish. It can be frozen pizzas or printer ink. But shoppers in this profitable frame of mind are looking for ways to minimize future shopping visits. Many warehouse retailers initially built their entire business model on the stock up trip. Shoppers spend more money and want larger package sizes on stock up trips. They typically evaluate the value of a deal over a longer period of time. Which means showing a price per serving or per use is a good idea to help them overcome the initial sticker shock on the price tag for a large item. They also need larger carts and more durable shopping bags.

Shopping For An Event – Shoppers who are shopping for an event behave differently than normal. A price-conscious dress buyer may throw caution to the wind when shopping for a dress for her daughter's wedding. Event shopping usually means that a shopper is more open to considering a "full solution." A shopping trip to select a swimsuit for a vacation can more easily include a cover up, sandals, tote bag and sunglasses. Shoppers project themselves into the event and usually appreciate suggestions for everything they will need. Events can be things like creating a nursery, bringing home a puppy or holiday entertaining. Adjacencies and full-solution merchandising is key.

Shopping For Someone Else – There are many situations where the shopper is not the intended end user of the purchase. It can be as common as a parent shopping for baby food or less usual like purchasing a gift. But the shopper is likely to make judgments and selections differently when they are shopping for someone else. They attempt to put themselves into the place of the person who will use the final item. Sometimes that is easy – like when a wife purchases her husband's usual shaving cream. And sometimes that is very hard – like when a grandfather selects a video game for a granddaughter. Merchandising and marketing can help reinforce messages so that the shopper can feel confident making their choice for someone else.

"Just Shopping" – As hard as it is to believe in today's busy world, shopping is also a pastime. Sometimes shoppers enter a store with no intention to buy. Call it curiosity. But they might enter a store just to see what is inside or to amuse themselves. These "just shopping" trips are opportunities to inspire shoppers with tremendous deals, creative displays and unique offerings. Shoppers may have more available funds than they let on. As a result, inspiring them with unexpected goods might mean they walk out with a hefty purchase.

One way to learn about your customers' shopping missions is to collaborate with the vendors and suppliers who usually do deep research into the psyche of category shoppers. (Usually referred to as shopper insights.) For example, pet food brands have deep experience examining the shopping behavior of a new kitten owner compared to a multiple adult cat owner compared to an owner with a cat reaching the end of its life. What they buy and how they make choices can become more predictable using shopping missions.

Another way to learn about shopping missions is to talk with your store managers and the people who work face-to-face with customers every day. They can tell you if they need more purple sweaters in Minneapolis (due to event shopping trips for Vikings games) or more cold canned soft drinks for lunch hour immediate consumption. Your store teams see shoppers and interact with them every day. Listen to their advice and learn to discern the different needs from neighborhood to neighborhood and the different shopping trips that drive shoppers into your stores.

Customer Decision Trees

So now that we have some good theory under our belt, let's talk about the reality of how shoppers make selections and how your merchandising can influence their purchase.

Retailers want to help shoppers see the breadth of products they could select from in their store. Then they want to enable the shopper to make their decisions easy. Shoppers typically employ several strategies to narrow down their choices within a category.

1. Price Point - Shoppers often start by setting a price range for the product they are looking for. They may consider their budget and look for products that fall within their specified price range. When this is true, merchandising by price bands can help them eliminate options that are too expensive or too cheap.
2. Brand Loyalty - Many shoppers have brand preferences in some categories. They may be loyal to a specific brand due to trust, quality or

previous experiences. When this is true, merchandising by brand will help them eliminate non-preferred brands and focus on products from within their favorite brands.

3. Product Attributes –Shoppers may have specific requirements for the product such as size, color, features, or ingredients. When you merchandise by attributes, shoppers can narrow their selection by eliminating products that don't meet their criteria. Shoppers choices are dynamic. Which is why retailers are continuously evaluating if a trend deserves its own merchandising position. Thus, some stores will decide to create a gluten-free aisle instead of interspersing gluten-free items across the store. Budget-conscious shoppers may justify a "dollar section" within your store. Understanding attributes that cross category divides and long-term trends can justify changes in your store merchandising.

4. Reviews and Ratings – In an age of online shopping and easy access to product reviews, shoppers may rely on the experiences and opinions of other customers. They may eliminate products with poor reviews or low ratings. Use of objective industry ratings (like Wine Spectator ratings) can be a helpful way to help shoppers who rely on reviews when making their selection. Even using a sign program like "employee picks" can be helpful. QR codes on product tags can direct shoppers to review sites to make big ticket purchases.

Category plans that put shoppers at their center have a logical flow of how shoppers consider making a purchase for that category. That is the customer decision tree. (CDT) Understanding how the shoppers narrow their choice, determines how to best merchandise the category. Your merchandise should intuit their process for reviewing the total selection, homing in on their most relevant.

Let's take mustard, for example. The customer decision tree may look like this:

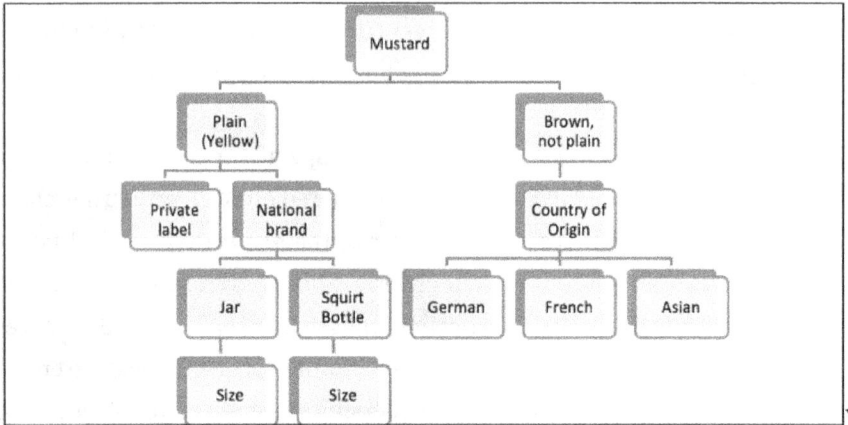

Figure 8: A Mustard Customer Decision Tree

This customer decision tree maps out the steps of a selection process starting at the top. Once a shopper decides to purchase Mustard, they will decide to narrow their choices to either plain/yellow mustard or a non-yellow mustard. From there, the choices for plain are to consider national brands or store brands. And then the package type. Presumably before considering size or price. For the brown mustards, the shopper usually selects country of origin next. Each of these levels and criteria is called a node. Shoppers have a preferred node for meeting their specific needs in that category during that particular shopping trip.

For shoppers, most purchasing trade offs will occur deeper down into the CDT. Meaning if a shopper wanted the national brand of yellow mustard in a squirt bottle, but it was only available in the 12 oz and not the 16 oz, it would be easier for the shopper to make that substitution rather than making a switch higher up in the CDT. This is sales transference. Smart retailers attempt to offer one or two selections at each node in the CDT to meet customer expectations but also to keep inventory and space as productive as possible.

Merchandising should similarly reflect the CDT so that shoppers can narrow their selections and make their choices at each step in the CDT.

Figure 9: A photo of a cereal presentation

In our example, cereal is purchased first based on whether primarily children, adults or the entire family will eat it. Which means merchandising should block children's cereals together, adult cereals together, and then cereals that appeal to everyone in the family together. In the photo above, children's cereals are along the bottom shelf. All family cereals are above, and the health-conscious adult cereals are on the top shelves. Cereals are presented within their subcategory by brand. From this, we could surmise that the following high-level CDT produced that presentation.

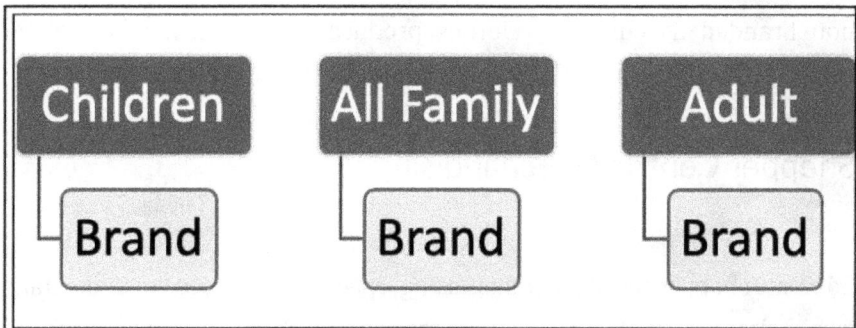

Figure 10: A Cereal CDT

Space Planners must understand the customer decision tree and the relevant importance of each node when developing a merchandising plan. The goal is to use this insight to make our stores easy to navigate and help shoppers quickly evaluate their options to make a choice.

Work with category managers, vendor partners and shopper insight reports to understand the CDT. Services such as Dunnhumby can create CDTs and help identify the exact items that are most likely to satisfy category shoppers at each node. Use that insight to create merchandising divisions (or blocks) that help shoppers navigate and home in on the exact item they want to purchase. By creating merchandising that aligns to shopper selection choices, shoppers will feel like your stores "get me." Building loyalty and long-term relationships with shoppers.

Because at the same time that they are making their purchases, they are also judging our stores. Are they clean? Are they inviting? Do they enjoy the experience? Or is it time that they try somewhere else? A lot is at stake in the short time they are in our stores.

Note that manufacturers and suppliers spend nearly all of their resources building brands. Which is why it is so common to see "brand" play an outsized role in center store categories. But in areas where products are non-branded like children's clothes, produce and electric wiring, look for color, quality and materials to play a larger role in customer decisions.

Shopper Centric Merchandising

To create shopper centric merchandising, space planners need to understand who their most profitable customers are and why. This is why it is important that Space Planning have access to the Shopper Insights (SI) that market research teams create. Once a space planning team can integrate shopper profiles with store profiles, they can begin to recognize and create the shopping experiences in the store merchandising that will most fully satisfy those shoppers. Simple insights into shoppers who regularly fill their pantries for multi-generational families versus harried shoppers who make frequent fill in trips during lunch hours, will lead to different store layouts and designs. Consequently, it is important that space planning teams have a full understanding of the target market, and that onboarding includes an immersion into who the stores most wish to serve.

To begin, shopper centricity in space planning begins with the floor plan. Planogram adjacencies should help shoppers make a complete purchase or at least consider their choices within a shopping mission. This is why disposable aluminum baking pans are usually in the baking aisle with flours, sugar and seasonings and not in the Paper goods aisle. People who buy baking goods are much more likely to purchase disposable baking pans than people purchasing trash bags or paper towels. The same is true with car cleaning solutions near replacement bulbs and wipers and not with the other household cleaning supplies. Understand category shoppers and their shopping missions to help drive category adjacencies.

One example of shopper-centric merchandising is the IKEA store design. Long ago, executives at IKEA decided that shoppers most want inspiration and ideas for how to live in their spaces and not aisles of chairs, lamps or dressers. IKEA uses vignettes to an extreme. The vignettes are not even near the stock to purchase. But the rooms inspire shoppers, and IKEA has trained its shoppers to select their products from the warehouse after seeing the vignettes. Is that shopper centric? Well, it's certainly inspiring and operationally efficient.

Can a retailer's intentions to serve shoppers go too far?

Plenty of US grocers have attempted to consolidate all the breakfast options into one breakfast aisle. Placing coffee & tea, cereal, and pastries in one aisle. Some have added refrigerated cases where milk, eggs, juices and bacon are merchandised. And many have seen their sales decline. Why? Because shopping habits move slowly. There is a general expectation built over decades that refrigerated sections are on the perimeter of the store. Frankly, because it is easier to stock and power than in the center of the store. Shoppers were confused by having some components of their list in the remaining perimeter sections (like butter and yogurt) while other components were in the center store (eggs and bacon.) In the end, most retailers have had to make operational choices ahead of their "shopper centric" merchandising. And while floor planners should be considering the likely shopping path of their targets, keep tethered to traditional routes and always test before committing to broadscale merchandising changes chainwide.

Visual Merchandising – Mastering The Art

L et's explore the three primary requirements for outstanding retail store space planning: the art, the process and the science. In every outstanding space team, there is a balance across all three to deliver appealing stores that are fresh to shop, easy to operate, and deliver outstanding productivity. Importantly, all three disciplines are necessary in every retail channel. So, whether you work in grocery, fashion, hardware or landscape supplies, these are the fundamentals that transcends all retail channels. Let's begin with the art of visual merchandising.

Solving Customer Problems

Good space planning succeeds for stores that sell pet supplies, lingerie, farm equipment and jewelry. The reason is that there are universal principles around good visual merchandising principles at retail. And whether you sell candy to Cub scouts or wigs to the wealthy, when you implement sound visual merchandising principles your customers will find your stores easier to shop.

Humans are very quick to recognize patterns – even if we are in a store we have never entered before. We are wired to find patterns and structure in the information that is constantly pinging away at us. Thanks to our neocortex and natural selection, the human brain is a pattern seeker. Understanding that gives great visual merchandisers two clear pathways to succeed: either lean into the pattern to make shopping feel as simple as breathing or disrupt the pattern to interrupt the patterning response in a shopper's mind to shock them into giving something a new look.

When we follow the first choice as merchandisers, our job is to take the range of products our merchants buy, the decision trees that describe how shoppers make their selection and make a merchandising pattern that is easy to decipher. No problem – right? Using Visual Merchandising principles helps.

Visual merchandising is the practice of placing products and fixtures in stores to create the most attractive presentation possible. It needs to halt a shopper and give them an emotional nudge. It might inspire them to create a funky dorm room, make a holiday meal or start working out. When a shopper is standing mere inches away from an item, how the product is displayed is the last and most intimate opportunity to influence that shopper's buying decision.

As customers shop to solve problems through their purchases. The problem may be that they need a fast breakfast for kids before school, a new outfit for a wedding or a greener lawn. But in every case, purchasing products solve a problem or resolve needs or desires. The purpose of visual merchandising is to provide an easy way for shoppers to imagine owning the product that will meet their need and then buying it. Clean stock, price tags that are easy to read, clear packaging all help customers make their selection. So do display models, mannequins, room settings and online kiosks. William-Sonoma is famous for cooking inside the store and letting the aroma waft out into the hall. What a great merchandising tool! Nothing makes shoppers imagine getting into the kitchen like the smell of fresh baked cookies or hot chocolate in the air.

Sure – customers have a budget for most shopping trips. But shopping is a combination of need, want and reward. Visual merchandising should help shoppers meet their needs —or create them! It should show them options that would satisfy their desires and make the selection process easy.

Artistically, space planners use their skills to create displays that are clean and attractive. Not just attractive in the sense that they are pleasant to view. But literally attractive in that they pull the shopper towards them. They use composition color blocking and creativity to make visually appealing presentations. With proper locations and adjacencies, they can influence where shoppers go in a store and how quickly they can navigate aisles. When visual merchandising is done correctly, the merchandising presentation helps shoppers sort through their choices and make their best selection.

Best practices in Visual Merchandising to attract shoppers, aligns to three key concepts:

1. Grouping products to support decision making
2. Grabbing the customer's eye with product blocking
3. Making it easy to shop

Great visual merchandising is like a silent sales associate. The products, their features and benefits along with their pricing should help a customer intuitively understand the range of selections on offer and help them make their purchase decision. Unlike a website with 5-star reviews, pages of description and videos of the product in use, a store must rely on the product's packaging and placement to help a shopper make their choice. It is always a bonus when a store employee engages with a shopper to help them, but space planners cannot rely on those engagements. The shelf presentation itself must help the shopper decide.

Attractive Organization

Here are common ways that visual merchandising helps shoppers make decisions:

Good—Better—Best Presentations

Good-Better-Best merchandising showcases a range of products to appeal to all customers. As a customer begins the "scan and shop" process, a Good-Better-Best merchandising approach can help them make a logical purchase decision.

This proven merchandising tactic begins with an opening price point item: a "basic" item. Let's say it is a plastic mechanical pencil. It contains one lead within the chamber, one eraser at the tip and could be refilled in the future. It is $1.99. The "better" item may include the pencil and a small container with additional lead and eraser refills. It is $3.49. Finally, there may be a much better version that is made of a higher quality material, plus the refills and a second pencil for $6.99. In this example, it is easy for the shopper to see how each step up in price, has a corresponding improvement in the product and its value. The customer will have to part with more money to purchase the "best" option. But it has a perceived higher value than either of the other choices. Placing the products in that order, helps shoppers make that connection.

The power of this strategy is that there is always a choice for the customer. There are selections for shoppers pressed for cash who need a lower-cost solution or for the customer willing to pay for a higher quality product. They can spend more to get more. That is why category managers like to offer at least three options of most items. It allows a customer to make a wise choice among the options that respects their needs and values.

There is nothing magic about having three offerings. In a product line that the retailer wants to dominate, there may be a dozen offerings. The important thing is to arrange the merchandising in such a way that the customer can easily see how stepping up and down in price generates a similar change in product features. Think of times when you have compared seemingly similar products at two different prices. Customers always wonder, "What else do I get for the additional cost?" When you clearly demonstrate the difference, you can carry a very deep selection of products in a single category.

When space planners need to display an edited, yet relevant selection of products, consider the Good-Better-Best merchandising approach. Make sure shoppers can easily see (through merchandising, signs and demonstration models) the increase in features with each increase in price. Begin with a basic model that has the minimum features your target customer needs at the right price. Present products that expand features up to the maximum price you believe you can command in the market. Make sure the presentation is clean – selection should either move from left to right across the shelves or up and down. Typically, when merchandised vertically, features and benefits (and price) increase as you move from bottom to top.

Eye-Level Presentations

Sadly, as customers, we are all a little lazy. As a result, products at eye-level (actually from hip to shoulder) tend to command the most planned – and unplanned - sales. As space planners that means that we can actually help our shoppers and our profits by deciding what goes on those predominantly shopped locations.

Here are two ways that space planners tend to use the valuable hip to eye shelf locations. They either place the most recognizable item in that space or the one with the largest market share. Those are key category signals for shoppers. They are usually the "anchor" items for their category. Anchor items are instantly recognizable and help customers navigate. Think of

Tide anchoring laundry detergent or Campbells Soup anchoring the soup section. They almost act as billboards that signal that a shopper is in the right location. Knowing that, space planners can use those key items to help shoppers navigates the aisle.

Another way to use eye-level presentation is to showcase an innovative or profitable item to the customer. For example, customers say they like to "try new flavors" of ice cream and snacks. But if they do not see them, they are likely to just grab their old favorites. Space planners can place new items and seasonal choices at eye-level so shoppers can find intriguing new items. The old reliables are still on display. Just not at eye-level. Retailers also use those prime locations to their advantage by placing their private or exclusive brands at eye level to make it easy for shoppers to purchase them.

Blocking

It can be overwhelming to navigate a store with tens of thousands of items. Blocking products can help shoppers make sense of the choices on offer. Suppliers purposefully create packaging that has a big impact when massed together. Brands are tenacious in selecting contrasting palettes in hopes that their products will stand out the most.

When color blocking, as a customer moves down an aisle, they are constantly scanning the aisle horizontally. Thus, vertical stripes or blocks tend to stop their eyes from moving. As they scan down the aisle, their eyes are arrested as they see vertical strips of orange, blue, red packaging. This is a tactics space planners can use to slow down a customer and cause them to process the selection and consider the items that are on view more slowly.

Nevertheless, perhaps no other merchandising tactics causes more headaches for space planners than "vertical brand blocks." Keeping vertical ribbons of products perfectly straight is almost always unrealistic. Both on the computer screen and in real life. When space planners create vertical brand blocks, there is almost always some degree of over- or under-compensation to help facings line up. But blocking can still be effective in smaller portions of the set. Consider how to block across shelves or only on the bottom or top half of the set. Then leave the rest of the set to wander a bit more.

Blocking is much more realistic on promotional displays. Suppliers cleverly use blocking in pre-built display shippers so that merchandising is easy and consistent.

Figure 11: Examples of blocking and the use of bold packaging color.

The Complete Solution

Visual merchandising makes it easy to buy the complete solution. The goal is to delight shoppers by giving them the complete package. That could mean an entire fondue set including Sterno® and cheeses. Or coordinated Christmas mantel and tree decorations. Or a camping set for beginners. Presentations should look to help a customer make their complete purchase in one place within the store. After all, there is nothing more frustrating than buying components for your dinner/entertainment center/bathroom only to get home and realize that something important is missing.

There are two ways to offer the complete solution in merchandise presentation: adjacencies and integrations. Adjacencies is important for floor planners who must consider which categories should share boundaries down an aisle. A common adjacency in the laundry aisle is stain treatments next to laundry detergents next to fabric softeners. Those are natural adjacencies for someone who solving a laundry problem. And they are all shelved on similar fixtures. (So even though cookies and milk go together as a "complete solution" they are rarely adjacent since one is refrigerated and one is room temperature.

Integrated solutions are when dissimilar items are on the same planogram. Vacuum bags are integrated into the vacuum planogram. Or antibacterial ointments are integrated into the bandage planogram. When these dissimilar items are combined into one presentation, it makes it easier for customers to anticipate future needs and purchase the complete solution. Retailers can induce incremental unplanned purchases since shoppers do not need to hunt for the complete solution across the store. Again, it takes advantage of shoppers' natural laziness to "pick it up while it's here" rather than search for the components in a future shopping trip.

Vignette

Visual merchandising that places products within their proper setting in the store is called a vignette. This is common in furnishings and household goods.

For example, when cozy bedding and coordinating linens are displayed on a well-made bed with stock for sale on adjacent shelves. Or mannequins wear complete ensembles that can be purchased throughout the department. Vignettes are when visual merchandisers create a carefully curated display or scene from product within the store. It is meant to draw attention and engage customers by evoking a particular mood or emotion. As such, it is a powerful tool to showcase products in an appealing fashion.

Vignettes usually include a theme or concept. Holiday settings in a winter wonderland, beachside vacations and sleek kitchen designs are vignette themes we have all probably seen. Vignettes often center on one color palette or aesthetic to keep the scene cohesive. No matter what, vignettes should be harmonious and focus on details.

Some stores have permanent alcoves or locations on the sales floor where vignettes can be built and changed seasonally. Many times, they are designed and directed like the front windows. Other stores take advantage of high traffic areas near entrances or intersections to showcase complementary products. One way to create a vignette is to pay attention to the lighting and the finishes in a particular area where collections will be on view.

Vignettes are meant to inspire shoppers and encourage them to explore and imagine. Shoppers find them immersive and memorable. Ultimately, they are a valuable way to drive sales by creating an emotional connection to the merchandise. They can build loyalty as a powerful tool to connect the merchandise in a store to its brand identity and values.

Merchandising in the Real World

These high-level principles are all well and good. But there are physical realities in our stores that the best space planners anticipate and resolve before sending instructions to stores

Understand the impact of shelf depths. Deep shelves are a fantastic way to maximize inventory holding power. But they can cast shadows on products below them – especially when they are shopped back away from the front shelf edge. When that happens, shoppers might believe there is no stock (since they cannot see the products tucked back and under other shelves.) To combat that, it is best to place large items on the lower shelves so that as the shelf inventory gets shopped back, the stock is still visible. The same thing can happen on high top shelves when packages are short. Taller items on the top shelf help make inventory more visible as shoppers select the most forward items from the top shelf

Create systems of organization for apparel. Hanging apparel should either be organized by style then size then color or by style then color then size. In any case, the shopper needs to be able to approach the fixture and quickly recognize how the product is being presented so that they can narrow their selection to the correct style, size and color. Be consistent throughout the department, so that once a shopper has deciphered your organizational method, they can quickly shop any fixture on the floor

Shop-ability is critical for peg board and slat wall presentations. Primarily use vertical blocks to organize product selections when merchandising on peg hooks. Larger items are always hung below smaller items. Customers must be able to grab products and remove them from hooks without colliding with other merchandise. Finger spacing around the products are critical to make it easy for customers to shop off peg hooks without knocking other products down. Most retailers require at least one inch all around the merchandise on a peg hook so shoppers can access what they want

Repeating patterns help shoppers find what they want. Use the same organizational rules when you merchandise a category. Do not merchandise Brand A buy size then flavor and then Brand B by flavor then size. Shoppers get frustrated as they stand in front of a section looking for an item that they "can't find.

Here is an example of that practice in action. Yummy Brand and Mega Brand have similar flavors and sizes. There are several different ways to organize the selection. The top example is by brand, then flavor and size. The next example is by size, then brand and flavor. The third is by brand, then flavor and then size. Any one of those arrangements can be decoded by a shopper. But the last arrangement follows one alignment for one brand and a different alignment for the second brand. So, a shopper looking for the "Mega Brand Chunky" item might be confused. It is a space planner's job to make sure that organization is consistent within a section

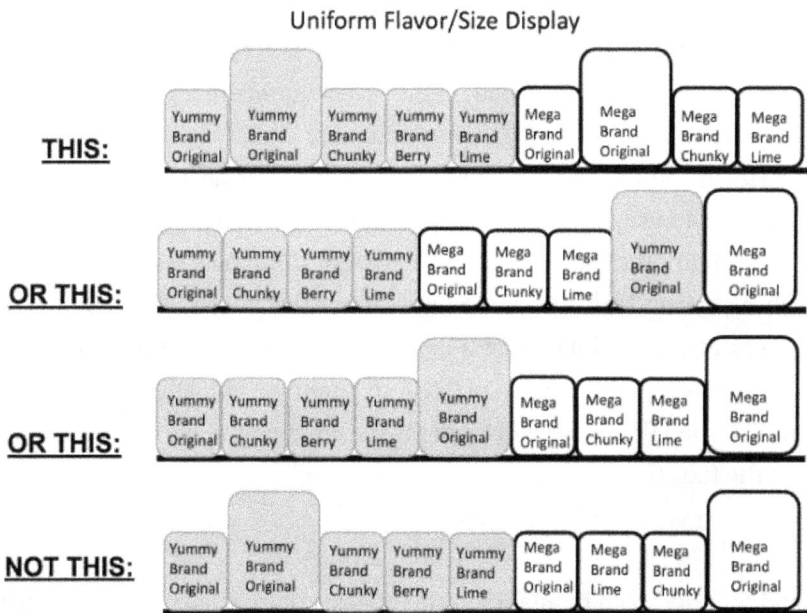

Uniform Flavor/Size Display

THIS:

| Yummy Brand Original | Yummy Brand Original | Yummy Brand Chunky | Yummy Brand Berry | Yummy Brand Lime | Mega Brand Original | Mega Brand Original | Mega Brand Chunky | Mega Brand Lime |

OR THIS:

| Yummy Brand Original | Yummy Brand Chunky | Yummy Brand Berry | Yummy Brand Lime | Mega Brand Original | Mega Brand Chunky | Mega Brand Lime | Yummy Brand Original | Mega Brand Original |

OR THIS:

| Yummy Brand Original | Yummy Brand Chunky | Yummy Brand Berry | Yummy Brand Lime | Yummy Brand Original | Mega Brand Original | Mega Brand Chunky | Mega Brand Lime | Mega Brand Original |

NOT THIS:

| Yummy Brand Original | Yummy Brand Original | Yummy Brand Chunky | Yummy Brand Berry | Yummy Brand Lime | Mega Brand Original | Mega Brand Lime | Mega Brand Chunky | Mega Brand Original |

Figure 12: A sampling of ways to uniformly merchandise products

Account for safety and security. It is the space planner's job to understand the anti-theft requirements for merchandising every item. Accounting for locking peg hooks, spider wraps and anti-theft boxes is the responsibility of the space planner when devising a visual merchandising plan. Space planners need to be aware of the following protocols that will impact their merchandising plans:

- Placing product into a locked fixture on the sales floor where shoppers will need assistance to access their purchase
- Using display models with stock cards where shoppers take a card to the checkout to represent an item available for sale from a secure location (back room or lock cage.
- Merchandising with locking peg hooks where a sales associate uses a magnetized key to release the product
- Hanging apparel with locking cables
- Place entire product lines behind the cash wrap where regulations require age requirements (like cigarettes or liquor.
- OSHA in the USA has defined requirements for aisleway widths and turning radiuses so that all shopping areas for the public are accessible by wheelchair. At least one cash lane in every store must be accessible by a wheelchair and provide a horizontal surface that allows a shopper to place their items on it while conducting a transaction. (Sometimes referred to as the check ledge.) There are OSHA requirements for anchoring fixtures to walls and floors depending on the fixture type and the weight of items on the fixture.

Beyond security, each retailer has their own set of merchandising standards. Ideally, there are written guidelines to follow. Common examples include:

- The maximum height for the top shelf to be set above the floor
- How high items can be stacked on a top shelf. Both of these standards are meant to make top shelves easier to shop safely
- Restricting glass containers from top shelves
- Overall restrictions for shelf capacity weight load

- Restricting heavy items on shelves below waist height
- Spacing products for "finger space" to grab items off the shelf. Making sure that there is enough space above an item so that it does not touch the shelf above it
- Weight restrictions for peg hooks and preventing pegs from being overloaded with items so they hang properly
- Hidden access to electrical outlets when there are powered display models to prevent injuries

Visual Merchandising creates a shopper's experience. That includes everything from the aroma from the bakery to the clutter in the aisles. People look at stores from different angles. A supply chain analyst will see a node that requires inventory. A pricing analyst will see a profit center. An operations analyst will wonder how efficiently it can be operated. A space planner needs to see the store through the eyes of the shopper. Notice if displays are too close together. If baby supplies are across from liquor. Notice if hand carts are stacked in convenient locations throughout the store when shoppers select more than they can carry. Notice if demonstration models are working properly.

When a visual merchandiser does their job correctly, the shopper enjoys the shopping experience. Items are easy to find and in a logical pattern. There are surprises that delight the customer along their journey that cause them to consider unintended purchases – just because the merchandising is so compelling. In other words, when visual merchandising is done well, it induces more sales. It is the silent sales associate that urges a shopper to trade up to a better product or purchase a complete solution.

But just as good visual merchandising encourages sales, poor merchandising can inhibit sales. When products are a jumble, it is difficult for customers to find what they want. Out of stocks are another issue. As the Harvard Business Review says: Stock outs cause walk outs. While there can be many contributing causes to stock outs, a planogram that is not properly balancing shelf capacity with customer demand is primary. Stores that are unkempt, unclean and disorganized are unlikely to meet customer expectations. The job of the visual merchandiser is like a home stager during a house sale: make that home as attractive as possible.

As we have mentioned, good visual merchandising helps customers visualize how products will look in their own home. But of course, they take up valuable space. Every kiosk, lifestyle sign, mannequin or demo unit that is placed on the sales floor displaces sales stock. While creating presentations, space planners must consider the value of the displays versus the stock it displaces. Consider keeping vertical brand stripes in perfect alignment. It is rare when the sales ratios align to perfect vertical brand ribbons. But visual merchandisers will make that tradeoff for crisp clean lines and store organization. Space planners must balance the visual impact of a large display instead of stacked boxes of inventory. Both tactics could be effective – depending on your shoppers and the products you wish to sell.

These fundamental merchandising principles work for all retailers: grocers, home improvement centers, shoe stores, pet stores. It doesn't matter. Each retailer will have their own requirements for merchandising. There are specifications that will be required to prevent theft or support the brand. But learning these principles and applying them will provide you with a solid foundation for your career in space planning – no matter where you go or what your stores sell.

Category Management– Mastering The Process

C reating a beautiful and appealing store environment will not matter if the retail enterprise struggles to move products smoothly through its operations. Space Planning plays a critical role in bringing new products to market. From the time that a buyer identifies an attractive new product until it is prominently displayed for sale, the space planning team enables everything from the first order to marketing the new product. For retailers who master the process, they capture the early excitement for new products and operate their stores and supply chain without disruptions. When space planners master the process, the entire organization delivers a better experience to shoppers and simplify life for the store team members who operate the stores.

For organizations following the category management process, space planning is one of the steps within the overall category review and planning process. While there are many variations, broadly, the review process aligns to this:

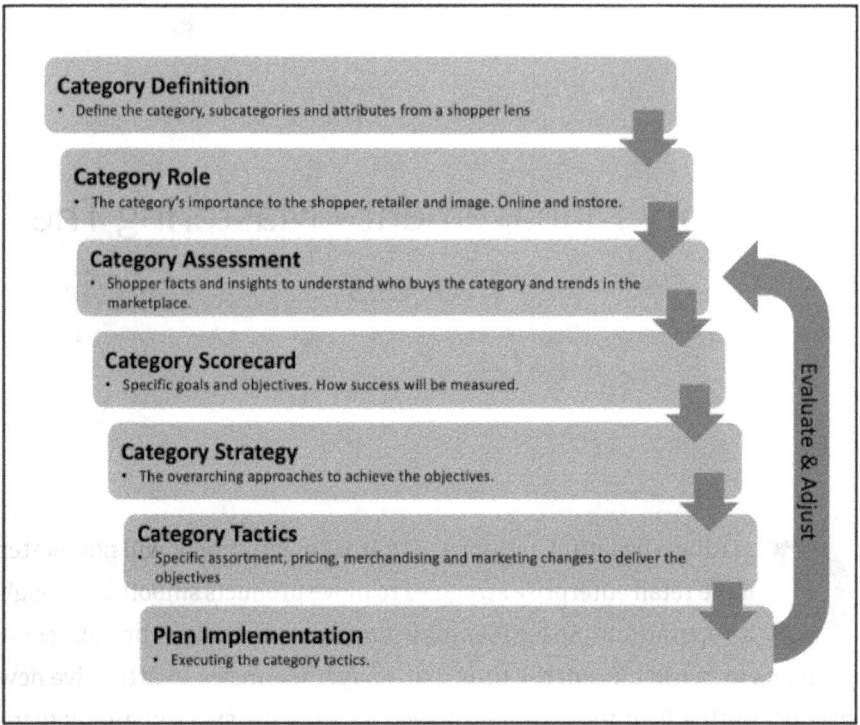

Category Definition
- Define the category, subcategories and attributes from a shopper lens

Category Role
- The category's importance to the shopper, retailer and image. Online and instore.

Category Assessment
- Shopper facts and insights to understand who buys the category and trends in the marketplace.

Category Scorecard
- Specific goals and objectives. How success will be measured.

Category Strategy
- The overarching approaches to achieve the objectives.

Category Tactics
- Specific assortment, pricing, merchandising and marketing changes to deliver the objectives

Plan Implementation
- Executing the category tactics.

Evaluate & Adjust

Figure 13 : An example of a category review process.

Within a retail organization the end-to-end duration of a category review process can be as short as ten weeks or as long as eighteen months depending on sourcing requirements, production timelines, category complexity and organizational agility.

There are several places where space planning plays an active role in the category management process.

First, there is an overview of how well the category as it is merchandised in the store aligns to the category as planned by the Category Managers. (CMs) Some retailers keep their financial planning category hierarchies and their merchandising or planogram hierarchies identical. Thus, when a CM plans the skin care category, it exactly aligns to the skin care planogram and space allocated for skin care throughout the stores. Other retailers have much looser alignment between the financial planning category hierarchies and their merchandising or planogram hierarchies. Which means a CM planning the skin care category may impact a portion of many planograms: the hand and body lotion, facial care, sunscreen, and first aid planograms. When that happens, it is usually up to the space planning team to provide a summarized reporting of the space allocation, item count by planogram and space performance analysis early in the process to provide the CMs with an understanding of how the category is merchandised in the stores.

At the earliest stages, there should be an analysis of how well the category is performing versus other categories in the department and balance of the store. Sales per square foot or GMROS (gross margin return on space) are the most common measurements. If a category is seriously over- or under-performing, it may justify a change in space allocation for the category as a whole. This is combined with market share data, shopper insights, trend forecasting and other data during the category assessment phase to help a CM create a differentiating plan for the category to meet the company objectives.

Strategically, there should be at least one interaction between the category managers and their space planning partners early in the process. This is when the CM can describe their major focus for the category and changes that they would like to make. This helps the space team get a sense for the timing and scope of changes so they can evaluate how they can support the changes. If there is a major new market entry or an important trend, the merchandising may need to be completely reimagined. If the changes will be minor adjustments, the merchandising may just need to be tweaked. During this meeting, space should reinforce due dates for all assortment changes so that downstream activities by the inventory allocation teams, DC's and stores can smoothly execute their parts of the process.

What to bring to a strategic planning meeting:

1. Current store count by POG
2. Current item count by POG
3. Major fixture outliers and variations (For example, 60% of stores have upright freezer cases while 40% have bunker cases would be helpful to know.)
4. Competitor photos of their merchandising designs with notations about fixtures, signage and product flow.
5. Charts or graphs showing performance by footage variations and other standard reporting decks used by your company.
6. Any known issues that are expected to be addressed during the planogram change.
7. Known chronic out of stocks,
8. moving a subcategory to its own planogram,
9. sign changes,
10. floor plan moves,
11. Product currently merchandised out of compliance with company standards
12. Finger space and shopability issues.
13. Any known agreements in place with vendors about contracted space or fixtures.
14. Any known items that are merchandised in a cut case, display unit shipped to store or other merchandising bundle that would prohibit reducing space for those items.

When the category manager discusses their strategies, listen for the things that a space planner can influence, like:

- Reducing out of stocks and lost sales – Which items are most at risk and can the planogram provide more shelf holding capacity?
- Boost exposure for a specific brand or new items – Could they have a more prominent location in the planogram?
- Improve inventory turns – Which items are dragging turns down and can

the planogram decrease their shelf holding capacity? Is there a different case pack available for the item? Could the DC select the product in smaller pack sizes? (Inner packs? Each unit?)

- Improve shop-ability – Are there items that are difficult to locate or select? Should there be a new merchandising system like pushers, gravity feed racks or dividers to make it easier to shop? Should there be more informational signage?
- Differentiate from (or align to) the competition – Review how competitors are merchandising the category and pivot away from (or adopt) their approach.
- Improve market basket sales – Is there a way to improve adjacencies or cross-merchandise selected items?
- Improve Private Label consideration – Is there a way to make comparison shopping easier for private label versus national brands through positioning on the planogram?
- Contracted agreements – Are there agreements in place with vendors to guarantee placement or minimum distribution levels?
- Special events – Is there a key holiday or event that is driving the change? What other departments will need to be involved to make sure the change is successful?

Remember that the category manager is likely to be addressing category tactics through many different lenses. They may be considering negotiating new terms with suppliers, changing pricing strategies, new sources, changing promotional plans, online positioning and many other ways to improve the business. It is your job to listen to their strategic goals and then interpret them into the changes within your control. It is rare to find a Category Manager with both the expertise and the time to translate all of their requirements to a planogram level.

The Assortment Handoff

Tactically, there are many ways to begin the actual planogram change work.

First, the CM will need to hand off a final merchandising assortment for the category. They need to provide direction about which items are to be discontinued, which remain, and which are new. They should also provide clear direction about which products should be in all stores and which ones are required in specific markets. This assortment handoff is also critical for the inventory team which must stop replenishment purchases for items being discontinued. The pricing team needs to determine if current purchase rates will consume the remaining inventory before the planogram change or if they need to begin a markdown process to escalate shopper purchases to eliminate inventory.

At the highest level, the assortment for any given planogram should capture the most customer sales as possible for each store. Looking at cumulative sales as well as unique offering range can help identify the optimal assortment limits for a planogram. While this is a simplistic view, it can be valuable in aligning on the items that should be considered for deletion.

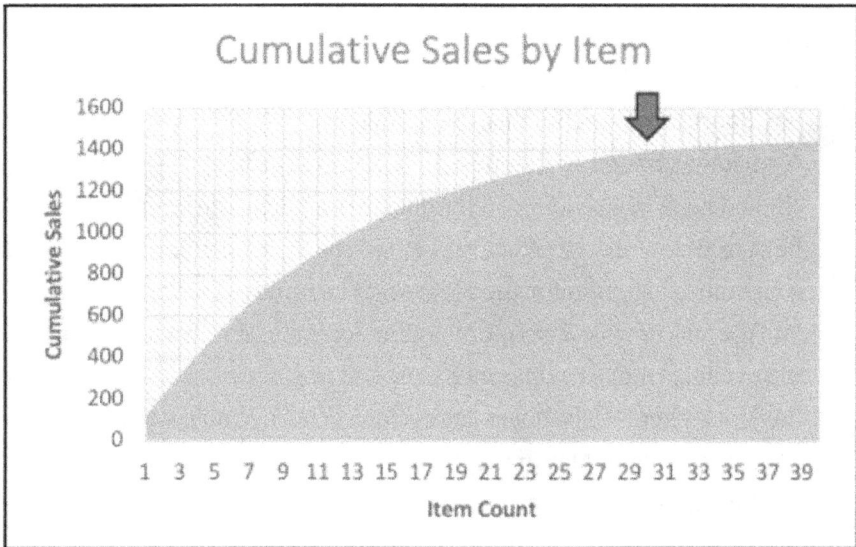

Figure 14: A Cumulative Sales Chart to pinpoint optimal assortment count.

There are several different reasons that an item change will need to happen during a planogram transition: : A Cumulative Sales Chart to pinpoint optimal assortment count.

1. A discontinued item – Either the vendor has stopped producing the item or the retailer has decided to no longer carry the item in any store. Remove the product from all planograms and inform the stores how to merchandise the remaining product. Inform stores if there is a new item that should replace the discontinued one or if adjacent items should expand to fill the space.
2. A new product introduction – A new item on the market OR a product that has existed int eh market which the retailer will now carry. Requires new direction about where it should be merchandised and positioned on the planogram.
3. A package change with the same UPC or item number – These changes usually do not require a change in merchandising placement on the shelf and past sales can usually be considered for future sales forecasts. Generally old items will simply sell out and the new items will replace

them. Often seen with seasonal products and flavors. Use the new image or description, inform stores and carry on. Stores do NOT typically get any hours to remerchandise these changes.

4. A package change with a new UPC or item number – Often called a "linked item." Depending on the degree of change, the item may need to be placed on a new location on planograms. Some vendors will support a clearance program for the old item to be replaced with the new item. Use the new item or description then inform stores how to merchandise old product (move to clearance rack, sell in place, return to vendor.)

5. A swapped item – The buyer has decided to change one item for another in the assortment. May or may not be merchandised in the same location on the planograms.

The assortment instructions can be very simple (all items go to all stores) or very complicated where a different segment of the assortment goes to different stores depending on the store demographics and planogram size. For many retailers the assortment corresponds to the size of the planogram. Thus, the smallest set sizes get the core assortment. The next larger planograms get the core assortment plus more. And the largest planograms get the entire assortment. This is sometimes referred to as the "nesting doll" assortment plan.

A way to think about this is that the:

1. **Core Assortment** is the smallest assortment and is planned for all stores
2. **Base Assortment** is the smallest assortment for a cluster of stores – and will usually have more items than the core assortment – but the base assortment will remain consistent for all the stores that share the same cluster designation.
3. **Enhanced Assortment** add additional items again and should reflect the proper assortment for each size of planogram within a cluster of stores.
4. **Localized Assortment** are the items that are planned for specific stores

or markets that have strong local brands and shoppers who are loyal to their local producers.

5. **Full Assortment** is all the items sold across the category across every store in the chain. It may not ever be found in the market – even in the largest of stores – if it includes regional or local items that can only be sold in specific markets.

A report to see the correlation between assortments, clusters and the planogram size is this:

Consistent Planogram and Assortment Line Logic						
Size	4' section	8' section	12'section	4' section	8' section	8' section	12'section
Cluster	traditional	traditional	traditional	urban	urban	rural	rural
Sku 1	X	X	X	X	X	X	X
Sku 2	X	X	X	X	X	X	X
Sku 3	X	X	X	X	X	X	X
Sku 4	X	X	X	X	X	X	X
Sku 5	X	X	X	X	X	X	X
Sku 6	X	X	X	X	X	X	X
Sku 7		X	X		X	X	X
Sku 8		X	X		X	X	X
Sku 9		X	X			X	X
Sku 10			X				X
Sku 11			X				X
Sku 12			X				X
Sku 13				X	X		
Sku 14				X	X		
Sku 15						X	X
Sku 16							X
Sku 17							X

Figure 15: An assortment plan using the "nesting doll" approach plus clustering

Here you can see that SKUs 1-6 represent the "core" assortment and all planograms/stores carry those items. SKUs 7-8 go to the next larger stores and SKUs 10-12 go to the largest stores. But we have added a common complication by differentiating between clusters of traditional, urban and rural stores. Those stores have slightly different assortment selections, but they still follow the nesting doll approach where each successively larger planogram contains all the items found in its cluster's smaller stores.

If you follow this method of assortment planning, ensuring that items are properly accounted for is not too difficult. Run a complete Item by Planogram Report and look for any inconsistencies in assortment placement before finalizing your project. When done correctly, the Item by planogram should reflect the logic in the example above.

Localizing the assortment adds still more complexity. There are two common causes for creating a localized assortment.

The first is the market importance of local brands that may or may not be distributed across the entire chain. Products like Vernors ginger ale in Michigan, Legal Seafood chowders in the northeast or Sweetwater beer in Georgia. To meet local demand, a localized assortment needs to merchandise important local brands in some stores and categories. Localized brands are crucial in some categories like salsas, beer, coffee, and ice cream. Other categories like first aid, paper goods and auto parts have nearly no local brands.

The second reason for localizing assortments has to do with the supply chain that a retailer uses. If a retailer uses a distributor to access products, it may find that it's east coast and west coast distributor do not provide access to the same items. But they may carry a substitutable "like item." Sometimes that is because the supplier purposefully markets different brand names in different places. The ice cream brand "Edy's" on the east coast is "Dryers" on the west coast. The same is true with Hellmann's/Best Foods Mayonnaise, Arnold/Brownberry/Oroweat bread, McCormick/Schilling spices and Mahatma/Carolina rice. Those items have different packaging and UPCs and need to have different distribution nodes and planograms to reflect that.

Sometimes, the distributor makes a choice to carry one item in one warehouse and another "like item" in another warehouse because they can get a better deal and feel the change will not impact customer demand. For example, if they carry a salad crouton, they may carry a Marzetti item in one warehouse and a Fresh Gourmet item in a different one. But they both meet the need for a resealable 5 oz bag of seasoned croutons. And can be placed in the same location on a planogram.

Finally, there are incredibly specific situations that might require store-specific assortments and planograms. The most common examples are in direct store delivered (DSD) beer, bread and snacks. Beer and alcohol must abide by legal regulations that can exist at the state, county, and city level. Those regulations can generate store-specific assortments. In general, DSD vendors are often given freedom to modify planogram facings by store to accommodate variations in demand across neighborhoods.

Store-specific assortments can also be created when a retailer attempts to generate customer-specific assortments by store. For example, a livestock feed chain may need to vary assortments of feed based on whether local farmers primarily raise cows, horses, sheep, rabbits, goats or chickens. Or apparel that reflects school colors and rivalries may need to micro-tune the assortment to ensure that the exact right colorways are merchandised in the correct store. University of Michigan blue and gold is not likely to sell in East Lansing – home of the green and white Michigan State Spartans.[5]

As a result, space planners and category managers need to strategically align to how the assortment will be planned and, thus, how the planograms will be created to support that plan.

While this may seem logical and hierarchical, it is anything but that. Retailers trying to meet and satisfy their shopper's demands, know that stores and markets can behave very differently. Understanding the customer decision tree and substitutability (sales transference or cannibalization) means that

---

[5]   Yes, I am a Michigan State University alum. No, I will never stop using this example.

assortments can vary greatly across shopper clusters. Instead of looking like a ladder (where small assortments build to bigger assortments depending on the planogram size), the assortment plans can look like a deranged checkerboard where items are selected or omitted based on shopper demand variations and local product availability.

Assortments may seem smooth and stepped when a CM can review items that are in 100% of stores, 80% of stores, 50% of stores, etc. But when reviewed at the planogram version level, assortments can vary widely from store to store – even when they have the same fixtures and set size. Let's dive into that.

Organizational Alignment and POG Processes

The most common reason for adjusting a planogram is to support an assortment change. Typically, the slowest selling items will be removed across all stores. Some poorer performing items will be removed from the most common planograms to only be placed in the largest stores or the stores with the highest sales volume. Blockbuster new items will go into every planogram. Less predictable new items may only be placed in selected stores until they can show a track record of success. Those decisions and directions should be a collaboration between the category manager, space planning team and inventory planning. Let's take a look at the reasons they are all involved.

The category manager creates an assortment that is most likely to profitably meet all of the expected shopper need states. Let's say there is a new dill pickle flavored chip. That is an extremely popular flavor in the Midwest, so the category manager says to put it in every planogram that serves Midwest stores. They also believe it could be appealing in the East, so they also direct it to go into the mid-size and largest stores in the east.

The space planners take that direction and begin to apply it to all of the planograms in the Midwest. In doing so, they point out that the new untested item will replace a very strong seller in the smallest stores. Before making such an impactful decision, the space planner will consult with the CM. The category manager may or may not agree on the dill pickle gamble once they review the sales in jeopardy for small stores.

As you can see, assortment and merchandising is not a linear process, but one that often cycles back for verification during the development phase. Seasoned planogrammers know when to make decisions and when to review choices with CMs. Experienced CMs know how to empower planogrammers with the strategic goals and financial reporting to make solid choices on their own. Together, the team is focused on delivering a unified vision.

Once the space planner and CM have placed the new item in as many planogram versions as they can in both the Midwest and the East, the inventory planners review the placements for alignment to distribution nodes. If the new product flows through the retailer's distribution centers, it will have to meet a minimum threshold of store locations in order to justify the space it will take up in the DC. If a DC were to service 45 stores in the East but only 2 of those stores get a planogram calling for the new dill pickle flavored chip, the DC slot may be too valuable to hold inventory for just 2 stores. The Inventory team may push back and ask that the item either be dropped for those two stores or be added into more planogram versions in the east. This can lead to more planogram re-work or even more planogram versions.

Once again, the process for properly merchandising planograms is a cross-functional cycle that may cause the development to loop more than one time before a final set of planograms are approved. That looks like this:

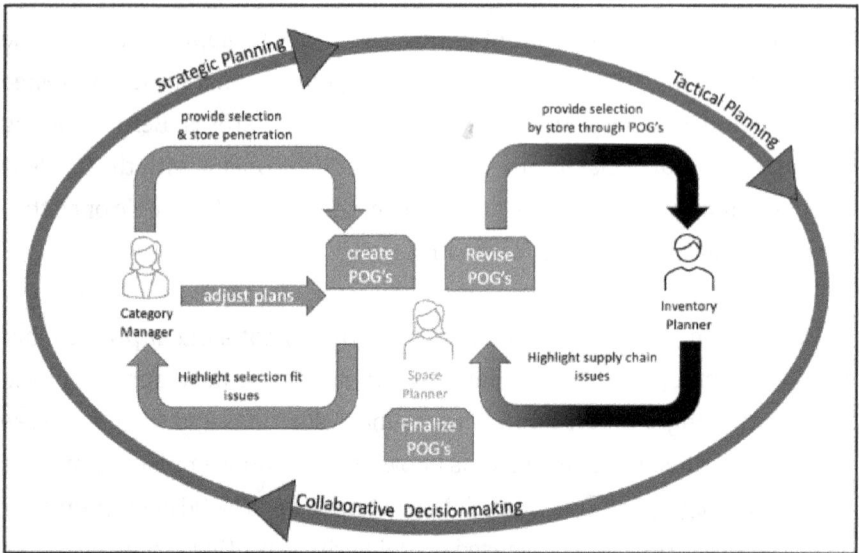

Figure 16: The collaborative planogram cycle

Because of the cycling nature of planogram production between category management and inventory planning, some retailers create category "pod's" where functional team members are co-located to facilitate ongoing collaboration. In organizations where each of the functions operate as separate entities, handoffs must be tightly synchronized to prevent disruptions.

One caution about assortment planning: Beware of over-assorted planograms. Chains can over-assort planograms when products will physically fit in the space, but the assortment is so broad that it does not operate efficiently. Products are under-spaced and the best-selling items regularly experience out of stocks because the shelf holding power is not high enough. Besides losing sales when fast sellers turn too quickly, the tore itself is more expensive to operate when store associates must continuously replenish the shelves. One of the most critical feedback elements for space planners is to continuously balance the category manager's desire to boost sales through larger assortments with the realities of store operations. Creating a partnership with inventory planning is helpful. As is creating an e-commerce strategy where an extended assortment is available online, but not in stores.

The Golden POG and the Planogram Lifecycle

Besides strategic alignment to the specific assortment plan, the category manager and space planner need to align to the overarching merchandising plan that will guide all planogram versions. Just as a floor planner uses a "block plan" for a store layout, aligning to a planogram's "block plan" helps build common understanding between the CM and space planner for the merchandising strategy. Look below to see examples of planogram block plans:

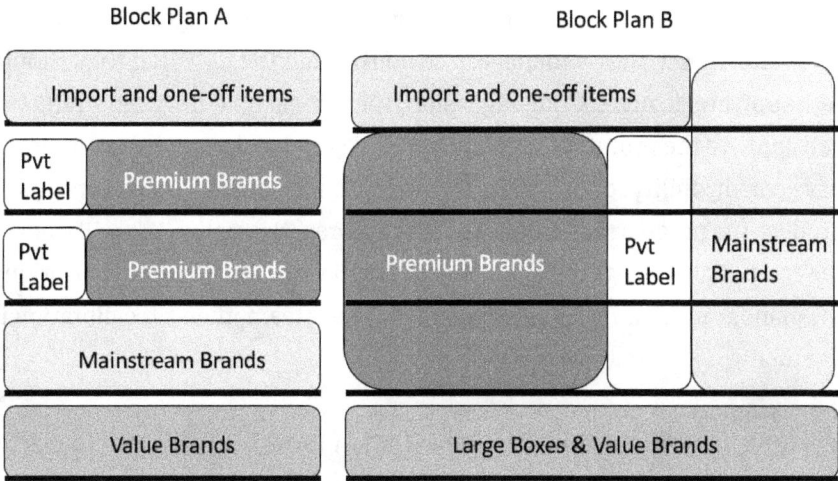

Figure 17: Examples of planogram block plans

Ideally the space planner will translate this block plan to the smallest, most common and largest planogram so the CM can see their vision in these "golden POGs" before they are executed in stores. Some retailers do all of this through digital images and approvals. Others have a mock-up room or space where the sample set is created with real products. Sometimes called the "walk through" this is a chance for all the interested parties to come together and provide their input into the merchandising scheme before planograms are sent to stores. People typically included in a walk through are the category management team, the space planners, category marketing team, loss prevention, store operations, store communications and inventory management. Optional attendees include suppliers, financial planners, fixture designers and IT, when appropriate.

There is a tendency in some organizations for category managers to nearly merchandise every planogram. Which is a poor use of time for both the category manager and the planogrammer. If you find yourself in a situation where the CM is scrutinizing each planogram, re-arranging products and perhaps making facing adjustments, this is a time to step back and recalibrate roles. There should be executive alignment from the divisional merchandise managers down through the CMs that they should set the strategic merchandising vision, the critical inventory requirements and approve the prototypical planograms. Then the planogram team should have responsibility for cascading that direction through all of the versions to produce the necessary planograms for the stores. Naturally, CMs will want to see and possibly nudge a few merchandising choices. But if they are "working the planograms" as much as the space planning team, then a recalibration is in order.

A way to think about this is to use a RACI. A RACI is a great tool to clarify who is responsible for each step along a cross-functional process. The RACI stands for:

R	Responsible	The team or person who is responsible for completing the step in the process. They "do" the task and execute it.
A	Accountable	The person who is responsible for the decision or the task. They have the authority to make a final decision. This should just be one person – not a team of people.
C	Consulted	These are the people who are needed for their input into the step in the process. They can provide input or feedback.
I	Informed	These are the people who need to be kept in the loop about the progress and execution of the tasks. They need some level of visibility.

While each organization will create their own RACIs to customize how the work is accomplished, a RACI framework for planogram creation looks like this:

	R	A	C	I
Select Assortments	CM	CM		IP
Define Merch Strategy	CM	CM	LP	
Set Inv. Thresholds	IP, CM	IP	SP	
Create Golden POG's	SP, CM	SP		
Approve Golden POG's	CM, SP	CM		
Create All POG Versions	SP	SP	CM, IP	
Send Inventory for POG's	IP	IP		SO, SC
Assign POG's to Stores	SP	SP		IP, CM,SC
Execute POG's in Stores	SO	SO		SP, IP, CM
Audit for POG Compliance	SM	SM	SO	
Correct Space Errors*	SP, SM	SP	SO, SM	

CM = Category Management

SP = Space Planning – could be Category Captains, in some models

IP = Inventory Planning

LP = Loss Prevention/Asset Protection

SC = Store Communications

SO = Store Operators – Could be 3PL, in some models

SM = Store Management

* A Space Error could include floor plan corrections for a store, changing a POG assignment or requesting a new POG version.

Each organization could have different teams involved and different steps in their unique process. But the important outcome is that a RACI is developed to reduce ambiguity about how work gets done across teams and who gets decision rights along the journey. When everyone knows their roles and responsibilities and there is consistency across all business lines, it is easier to improve efficiencies and provide clear communication.

As the category process moves from strategic to tactical, plans must be complete and accurate. Validations and checkpoints are key to making sure that projects are error free. Typically, planograms follow a life cycle of refinement as they make this journey.

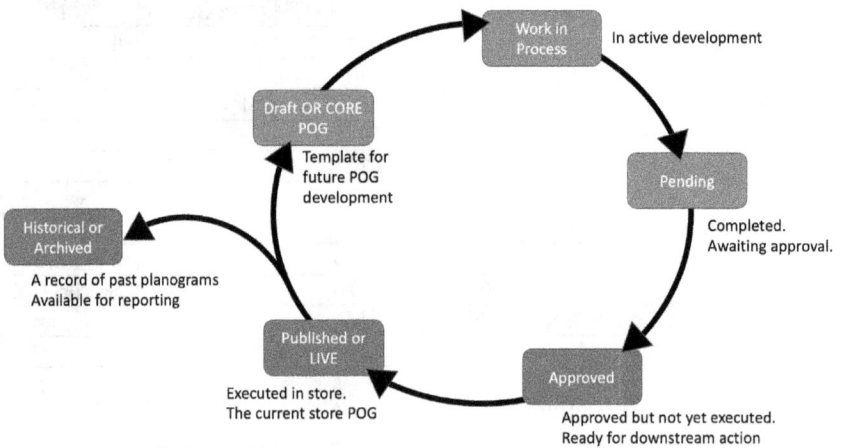

Figure 18: A planogram (or floor plan) lifecycle and status changes.

Changes are not made after "Approved" status. Files must revert to an earlier status to be editable.

First a planogram is *In Draft* status. This may begin with the Golden POG or POG template that is unlikely to be sent to a store to be executed. The POG in this status serves as a communication device to build alignment before all of the versioning begins.

Next planograms attached to the category go into *WIP* status (Work In Process/Progress.) Planograms stay in this status as the old items are deleted, new items are added, and the placement and facings are optimized to account for sales velocity and minimum inventory requirements. Once the planograms in WIP are completed, they can move to *Pending* status.

In *Pending* status, the planograms are awaiting approval. Approval may come from a CM review, a store operation review or an internal space planning review. In any case, this is the last chance to adjust the planogram before action is taken on the category's future merchandising plan.

Once the *Pending* planograms have been approved, they move to *Approved* status and data starts to be shared cross-functionally for action. Discontinued items or items that will be carried in fewer stores after execution are communicated to suppliers for their internal forecasting. Replenishment orders cease or are adjusted. DC slots are emptied and repurposed. Store pricing may change and clearance markdowns may begin. New forecasts are generated for new items or items expanding distribution. Orders are placed. Store instructions are created. New store pricing labels are generated and printed/shipped, if required. New fixtures are ordered. New signs are created. Store execution labor is scheduled for the week of the transition.

Finally on the week of the transition, the *Approved* POG becomes a *Published* POG. That is the official transition date for the planogram and will mark the point in time when the new assortment and new planogram will be measured for scorecarding.

Note that:

1. A POG does not have to be in a "published" status to allow stores to see a preview of the planogram changes that will be happening in their stores.

Settings can be adjusted so that stores can see the "pending" POG at Publish date minus two weeks, for example. This allows store managers and operators to see the scale of the changes and plan accordingly.

2. If a store does not execute the planogram transition on time or if new items do not arrive on time, the space productivity for the category can degrade. Imagine if you were a CM and you had a financial plan for new items were going to generate an incremental +10% in sales upon POG transition. If the stores are delayed in setting the planogram, each week reduces the chance for meeting that plan.

Finally, old planograms that have been removed from store directions are usually saved as *Historic* or *Archived* planograms for reporting purposes. They may remain in the database for years.

Planogram Change Tactics

Generally, planograms will belong to a project. That project may be June 2025 Baking Mixes or Ocean Fishing Supplies Spring 2025. But there will usually be several planograms that need to be updated at once. Planograms typically tie assortments, floor plans, merchandising hierarchies and sales volumes together in one shared file. To that end, planogram names usually carry a great deal of information in them and adhere to a strict naming policy.

Here is an extreme example:

Dept Number		Width	Depth	Cluster		Kickplate height

071_BAKMX_12_066_24_NE_S_7IN

Floorplan Short Name		Height		Volume Group

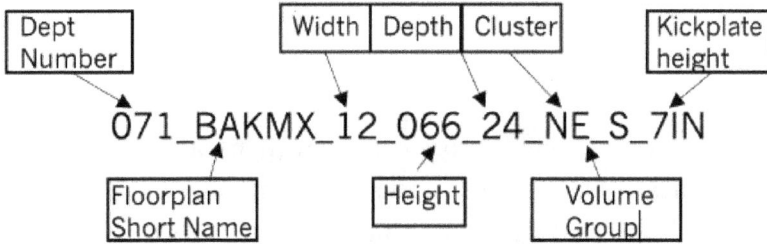

One of the most critical connections is between the planogram name and the floor plan identifier that is used to "place" the planogram on the floor plan. Sometimes it is a name (as in the example above) and sometimes it is a complete floorplan location ID when the planogram is store specific. In any case, it is critical to strictly adhere to the planogram naming convention that has been set up by the retailer to retain connectivity across multiple systems and allow for accurate space reporting.

Depending on the software and implementation, there will be a sequence of steps to open the planograms in the project, import the new assortment(s) for those planograms, delete the discontinued items, add new items and then merchandise the planogram. We will not go into that here because there are so many instances that each have their own protocols depending on the systems and the integrations.

But once the planogram assortments are updated and applied to each planogram, the two critical steps are to merchandise the planogram to be as attractive as possible. The planogram should follow the customer decision tree and merchandising guidance that was given during the strategic planning meeting. Then the planogram needs to be adjusted to support the inventory requirements to meet all sales demands and minimum shelf inventory requirements.

As you remerchandise a planogram, consider that sales and profit are important for positioning and placement. While unit velocity is the most critical metric when balancing facings and space allocation. A unit sold equals a happy customer. Whereas a dollar sold may only be a fraction of a happy customer.

With discontinued items removed and new items added to the set, first adjust facings to address out of stocks. (Please review Chapter 7 Analyzing: Mastering the Science for more on using proper performance measurements.) You may "overflow" shelves in this step. That is okay. Because in the next step, you will reduce over stocks. Now you should be able to see which fixtures have space available and which ones are overfilled. Make the proper merchandising adjustments to balance inventory across all fixtures on the set while adhering to the overarching merchandising direction. Block your planogram as much as possible to adhere to the customer decision tree. Try to create brand billboards throughout the set. Or repeat brand and product ribboning. Be consistent in flavor and size placement across all brands to make it easier for your customer to recognize patterns and find what they are looking for.

Finally, make tweaks wherever possible to address issues that came up during the strategic planning meeting. If the category manager wants to emphasize choice and variety, consider keeping items even if it limits the shelf holding capacity. If the goal is to fight chronic out of stocks, add facings to best sellers to provide additional safety stock. Take care to showcase your private brands properly to either emphasize their affordability or their feature set. Continuously review the planogram for inventory problems.

To see that, highlights are a great way to visually pinpoint issues with blocking and inventory imbalances. Highlights change products to a different color and provide a legend so that users can quickly review their planograms. For example, a brand highlight can pinpoint any errant items that have strayed from their brand family while merchandising the set. A Days of Supply highlight can identify items that have too much or too little inventory which can be adjusted by changing facings or merchandising styles

Commonly used highlights in planogram merchandising and reviews include:

Duplicate UPC: highlights any items that are merchandised in more than one location on the planogram.

Case Pack Min: highlights any items that are merchandised to hold less than 1 case of product on the shelf. (or some multiplier of a case pack. A 1.5 case target is common.

By Brand: allows users to see brand block.

By Manufacturer: allows users to see manufacturer block.

Private Label: allows users to see where private label items are merchandised.

Adds: highlights new items added to the set.

Top 10: highlights the top 10 items by sales, volume or profit.

Spectrum: highlights the items from top to bottom on a selected metric using a color spectrum.

Changes: highlights items that have changed their facings, position or merchandising style during the planogramming session.

Warning: highlights items that have violated a merchandising rule such as a fixture collision, finger space, products that overhang the shelf edge, ineligible fixture merchandising (pegged items on a shelf, for example.) Or fixtures that have violated rules like shelf placements that are not in the notches of a back board or are set too high.

Using highlights and adjusting merchandising all happens while a planogram is in the Work in Process stage. Once the planogrammer has completed their work and believes that it is ready to be reviewed, they can change the status to "pending.

Here are some of the things to check when you are about to move your planogram to pending to ensure that you are completing a high-quality planogram:

• Fixtures are accurate and align to the previous planogram or include approved fixture elements for the project.

- Shelf depths are correct. No shelf is deeper than the shelf below it.
- The top shelf of your planogram is at the same height across all segments of the planogram.
- Special racks, dividers or signs are properly accounted for.
- The base deck or kick plate is set correctly. Base decks are the same for the entire width of the planogram.
- All peg hooks are the same length (depth.)
- All shelves are set back to a Z of zero. Meaning that they are properly aligned to the back of the backboard. (View in 3-D to get visual confirmation.)
- All assortments are consistent in the project.
- All unallocated products have been removed from the planogram file.
- Remove/replace any placeholders or text boxes that were create dot stand in for products on the planogram.
- Crush or squeeze is accurately applied.
- All dates are correct.
- Stores are properly assigned to the planogram.
- Planogram is named properly.

Finally, before turning over your planograms for approval, it is common to create a before and after view of the work you did. You may have a project or a planogram scorecard that compares two versions of the work side by side. There are standard internal reports that come with planogram software packages and custom reports that your team may use. Expect to see measurements that compare expected sales, volume and profit, days of supply, product density measurements, gross profit percentage changes, inventory turns and inventory costs.

The Combination Planogram Dilemma

In small stores, it's common to see a retailer combine multiple categories onto one planogram. Consider a retailer who may combine nut butters with jams and jellies on 1 planogram. Or who places baby food, diapers, wipes, baby bath products and formula in one "baby" section. These combination planograms are treated the same as every other planogram change if they are planned and reviewed on the same cycle.

But what happens when diapers and wipes are bought by the paper CM while all other baby products are bought by a grocery CM? Or when nut butters roll up to condiments and jams and jellies rolls up to baking products which are on separate review schedules.

When combination planograms are managed in different cycles, the same planograms can end up in multiple life stages at once. The nut butters team may have the combination planograms in a pending status (approved but not yet published) at the same time that the fruit spreads project pulls those planograms in to "work in process' status. Besides the re-work this causes for the planogram team (to open and work a planogram many times over successive weeks) there are downstream impacts to buying, allocating and replenishment settings that can get triggered multiple times. Reporting can be unreliable when reports are meant to generate only off of planograms at a certain life stage, for example.

There are several ways to control this common problem.

First, is to look for a handful of invasive or wandering items and consider re-categorizing them. For example, if 4-6 cans of breadcrumbs are categorized in the bread department, but they are always merchandised in the baking mixes, then moving them (and their historical sales) into the baking mix category and shifting responsibility for their merchandising to the baking mix buyer may be the right thing to do. This is most common where there are a limited number of products violating the merchandising hierarchy and they are always merchandised away from their home category's location. These "wandering/invasive" products are easily managed with some category re-structuring.

But when there are situations where some stores have items in one planogram while other stores house those same items in a different planogram, the solution is more complicated. Take a pet store that has cat food, cat treat and cat litter planograms. Each of those categories and planograms have different planning cycles. But in some very small stores, all three of those categories have one shared planogram. In that situation, harmonizing the planning cycles so that they are concurrent is the best way to resolve the root cause of the issue. If that is not possible, there are other ways to manage the complexity of combination planograms.

Combination planograms can adhere to a strict shelf count rule. Thus, whenever different categories on different planning cycles share a planogram, they can only be merchandised on full shelves. A category manager can then consider the precise selection they want to merchandise when they are limited to one-, two- or three-shelves on a combination planogram. This allows the CM to make a "space aware" decision while directing the assortments that ought to be on a combination planogram. Otherwise, a CM could substitute five new items to replace five discontinued items without realizing that they belong on different planograms in a store.

When combination planograms are limited to a full shelf mandate for shared categories there are advantages and disadvantages. The advantage from the viewpoint of the planogram and the store execution team is that they only have to "touch" certain shelves each time. They don't have to worry about resetting the entire planogram with each category's assortment changes. The disadvantage is that either business could be under- or over-optimized if what they "deserve" is a half of a shelf more or less than they are given. Also, as business dynamics change over time, the category balance can shift dramatically. A jams and jellies plus peanut butter planogram can be disrupted when almond, cashew and pecan butter sales accelerate, for example.

Combination planograms make macro space analysis very complicated.

Because measuring macro space usually matches category sales to category space, as categories are spread across many different planograms, keep data integrity high is difficult. (This is true whether the analysis is at the category, subcategory or any other hierarchy level.) Combination planograms make "top down" analysis nearly impossible and requires a "bottoms up" granularity at the item, store, location level. That can quintuple processing requirements and bog down all but the heartiest systems when a chain may have over 5,000 stores and 60,000 planogrammed items.

A systemic way to overcome combination planogram reporting difficulties is to implement a master data system where items can roll up to different hierarchies. It allows all stores and all items to roll up to one financial hierarchy (where all canned beans roll up to canned vegetables, for example) for standard category reporting. But then each item can also roll up to another *merchandising* hierarchy (where half the stores have all canned beans roll up to canned vegetables, but the other half of the stores segregate refried beans to roll up to Mexican food and cannellini and garbanzo beans to roll up to Italian food, because that is where they are merchandised in half the stores.) This approach supports a reporting system where every store can have its specific merchandising reflected in its performance data.

For store tests, secondary hierarchy reporting makes it much easier to evaluate whether merchandising changes are successful when evaluated against standard merchandising across stores. It supports store-specific macro space optimization analysis. It allows for easier omnichannel reporting when site users can navigate to the same item through multiple paths. It is especially useful when a merger or acquisition happens where each former entity categorized businesses differently. But it requires IT and systems support to implement and can impact every report user as they will have to learn how to properly submit queries to get the data back in their intended format. But this is reasonable table stakes for most modern merchandising systems.

Off Cycle Changes

This process presumes that there is a planogram calendar and that the assortment and merchandising changes align to a pre-defined schedule. But there are conditions where a category needs to have an adjustment that is not on its planned change cycle. Whether it is a change in a supplier, a critical new item launch or a regulatory adjustment, space planners must be ready to respond to requests for off cycle changes.

First, there should be a standard process and pro forma to ascertain if the off-cycle change is reasonably going to pay for the cost of the change. Consider using the "Off Cycle Planogram Change Pro-Forma Template" in the Appendix to see how the timing of the change, the expected sales increase, and the cost to make the change interact. This is a standard good practice for retailers who want to be objective when deciding which off cycle changes are supported. Of course, there can be outstanding reasons to conduct a change even if it will be margin adverse. For example, if there is a long-term out of stock and customers are frustrated and abandoning shopping visits. Or if there is a regulatory reason to change.

First off, one of the easiest ways to support off cycle changes is to plan that they will be necessary each month. In your annual budget, plan for a need for extra planogram production and execution capacity. If your normal change schedule requires 40+ hours of scheduled work from each team member to meet the schedule, it will be difficult to find excess capacity to make last minute changes.

The other is to limit off cycle changes to swaps or in-and-out changes that can be automated. While it will not alleviate workload at the stores, it will make production swift and instructions to stores simple to understand.

The Pricing Handoff

One of the most critical connections with space planning is the pricing in each store. While a strategic pricing team will work with the category managers to set every day and promotional prices, planogram changes drive several critical tactical pricing changes in each store.

First, there are the discontinued products that are removed from the shelves with a planogram change. The pricing system can gain visibility to exactly which items in which stores will be discontinued when a planogram is in the "approved stage" (see Figure 18.) Usually, replenishment orders to that store halt immediately. The pricing team can begin to activate a markdown cadence for the items that will be discontinued with the planogram change. The idea is to begin price reductions so that the store's inventory is as close to zero as possible on the execution date.

Based on the amount of inventory on hand in the store and the sales velocity, the markdowns can be passive or aggressive. A passive strategy makes sense when there are small volumes in the store and a high sales volume. Simply leaving the item at normal pricing and letting natural shopper demand reduce the inventory may be enough to liquidate the inventory before the reset date. An aggressive strategy happens when the store's inventory is higher than the expected natural shopper demand before the reset date. In that case, a closeout markdown begins where the price may be reduced by 20%, 40% and then 75% in hopes that the attractive prices will induce shoppers to buy more than forecasted to reduce the shelf inventory. If that fails, the products may be moved to a clearance outpost on the date of the reset, destroyed or returned to a vendor or DC.

The other link between the space planning and pricing system is to activate new items in the POS terminals for each store in advance of the reset date. New items that will be available for purchase in each store need to be matched to their pricing zone (if the retailer practices zone pricing) and each store must have the correct price set up in the POS system for every new item that will be added to the store's inventory.

On a more tactical front, the space planning system and the planogram positions typically activate a complete price ticketing print job. As part of a planogram reset, it is common to remove all old price labels from the shelf edge and replace them with new price labels during the reset. This ensures that the complete section is refreshed. To make this process as efficient as possible, space planning systems connect to price label printers to create store-specific label sets that have the accurate price for each item in each store and prints in the exact order that the items will be placed on the shelves. Whether the job is done centrally then distributed to all stores or if each store's print job occurs onsite, the planogram controls the order of the labels so that the people executing the planogram can simply place each product's label in order. This step saves hours in a large reset.

In some retailers, the labels are not individually printed. Instead, each shelf strip is printed as one continuous pricing label strip. In that case, the space planning data is even more critical to align the price directly under each facing. Because the spacing between each product's price labeling will be exactly what the space system precisely calculated for the number of facings for each product on the shelf. Hence, if a line of products are all in three-inch-wide packages and each product has two facings, every price label will be spaced exactly six inches apart on the shelf strip printout. Some retailers take this even further and print life-size pegboard backers that reset teams tape to the pegboard then fill as shown. Talk about making execution foolproof!

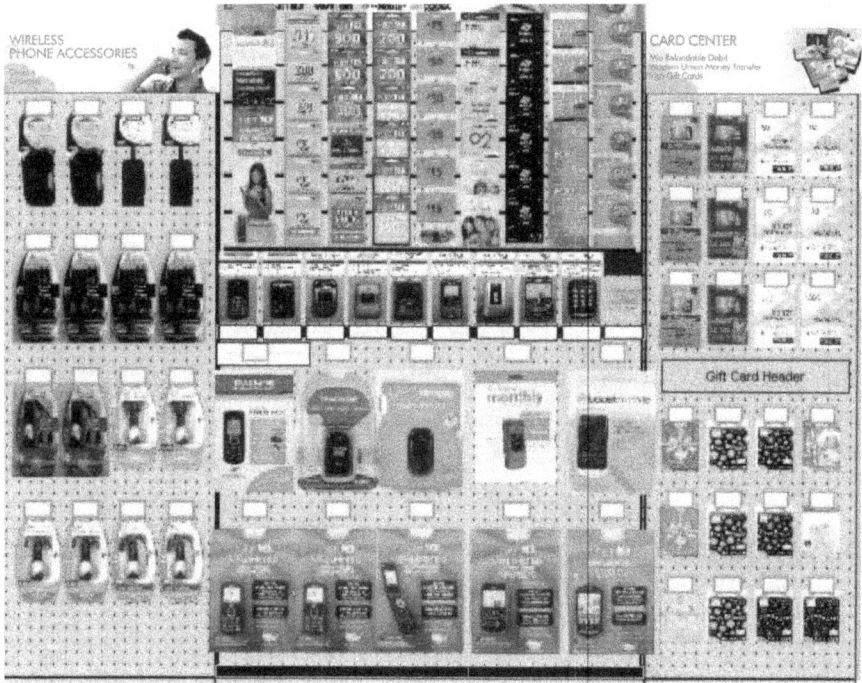

Figure 19: An example of a full-size pegboard backer for merchandising.

Next Level Collaboration: Your Supplier Partners

The effort to maintain and update every store's planogram version is usually beyond what a retailer can afford to resource. Many retailers use a Category Captain program to augment their internal staff and provide category-specific insights to create more productive store presentations. In an arrangement where two different companies share in the outcome of a complicated, time-bound process, there are many ways to fail. But there is only one way to succeed.

Be clear. Be consistent. Be predictable. Be respectful.

When you find yourself working with a partner, remember that everyone appreciates full transparency. Most issues arise when one side fails to accurately convey their true situation. With that in mind, start by being the person that always provides the truth. About dates, deadlines, expectations and deliverables. If you are working across a supplier (vendor) and a retailer, here is what to expect:

Retailers never move as fast or as far as suppliers want. They are constrained by competing initiatives and demands for store resources. They are balancing the need to operate an entire store and not just optimize a single category or department. They succeed when they have consistent execution across hundreds or thousands of locations and not excellent execution in some stores and minimal execution in others. Retailers and the people who work for retailers are not dumb, purposefully difficult or antagonistic. They likely have restrictions you are not aware of.

Suppliers always want to do what is best for their brands and company. While they may be as objective as possible to help a retailer drive overall category performance; at the end of the day, they want their company to succeed. With that bias, will always come some close calls that are made for the benefit of their company and products. Suppliers and the people who work for suppliers are not sneaky, uniformly discriminatory or free labor. They are partners who are looking for ways to make everyone happy. Not the least of which are the shoppers and customers who use the products.

So how can these fragmented players come together to deliver a high-quality shopping experience in the stores?

First, be proactive in communicating when planogram and merchandising changes are scheduled for stores. Then make sure that resources across both teams share a timeline to meet the changes. New items must be reviewed by category managers on time. Current planogram and performance files must be shared on time. Current performance must be analyzed to make recommendations before work begins. Perhaps no quicker misstep occurs than when suppliers want or expect stores to change outside of the standard calendar. (see off cycle changes.) Establish open and transparent communication pathways and escalation points. Create weekly or even semi-weekly updates so that everyone stays informed of new developments.

Second, provide added value to every step of the process you are involved with. Make your partners aware of store conditions you have documented. Address out of stock and new item availability issues so that the merchandising plans can be built to manage outliers. Provide insight to shoppers derived from loyalty programs or primary research. Give leading edge insights so that the merchandising changes can be as effective as possible from the very first day of the reset. It is frustrating to learn that a competitor had the jump on breaking news or trends and implemented a change that could have been addressed in a normal change cycle, if it was just known earlier in the process.

Another way to add value is to do establish KPIs. Everyone needs to be clear about how the two companies will measure success. If a project executes on time, but project milestones were missed and heroic efforts happened to reach the reset date, was the project successful? Conduct additional analysis or synthesize the information in a new way to draw new conclusions. For retailers, that means sharing new insights about adjacent category performance, aisle or department trends or other macro changes that a supplier working on one category cannot know. For suppliers, that means crunching the numbers when a retailer doesn't have the time or resources to do so. And distilling those analyses into actionable recommendations. If a retailer doesn't have time to conduct the analyses themselves, they probably don't have time to go through a deck of several dozen pages to uncover the insights you want them to see.

Third, reflect reality. Sometimes there are plenty of good ideas surfaced in joint business planning meetings. But when you see those ideas in a store environment, you may realize that it cannot be scaled or executed well. When different constituencies come together and try to build a common plan to meet everyone's needs, take the time to give it a strong reality test. Too many times expensive new fixtures, sign packages and custom development is done at scale without a proper test. If that happens, most of the time it is the supplier who has to eat that cost. Do everyone a favor and test new ideas in stores or mockup rooms and evaluate it thoroughly before making commitments.

Fourth, regiment your resources and your data to enforce confidentiality. Both parties will be sharing data that they value and legally need to keep secure. File sharing sites need to be encrypted. Resources should not work alongside multiple competitors (or near competitors) on a project. Be vigilant and ask tough questions about how data is partitioned. Expect regular IT screening and security audits. If you work as if every night could be a surprise audit, you will develop good habits in securing data and equipment.

Finally, keep your promises. 'nuff said.

In the past, for suppliers and retailers to work together on space planning projects, they needed to share the same software platform. Minimally, they had to be able to save and read the same space planning file format. Usually, that was a .PSA file for planogramming and a .DWG file for floor planning.

But in the future, as more solutions become SAAS (Software as a Service) and applications and data sets "live in the cloud," there is more opportunity for retailers and their supplier partners to work in the same space planning instance. With proper authorization, suppliers (and contractors) from around the world can log into a retailer's space planning instance and work directly in the same tool as the retailer's own team. To do that properly, vet suppliers and set permission levels to prevent them from accessing other categories or data that are not meant to support the project. Retailers and suppliers who integrate in this fashion can eliminate days of translation into and out of the retailer's native space plannings system when jointly creating a new project.

Share what you know. Integrated teams have the most potential to teach one another new methods and gain new skills. When each side understands one another and the challenges they face, it can be like having access to a whole new group of cross-training gurus. To ramp up learning and growth, conduct formal (or informal) reviews to identify where there could be improvements in the future.

Next Level Collaboration: Your Store Partners

All good space planners spend time in stores. If you are behind your keyboard most of the year, you will only improve up to a point. Sure, you might learn more quick key shortcuts. Or a new macro. But to deliver for your stores and your customers, you need to go out to see more stores.

Which stores to visit?

Ideally, you will have a chance to visit all your stores in your career. But at the very least the most critical stores to see are:

- The prototypical stores that represent most of the stores in the market. Look for examples of the stores that were opening during your chain's biggest expansion. Look for the floorplans that represent those stores. Not just the size (45,000 sf) but their shape and traffic patterns. Are most of your stores are narrow and deep? Wide and shallow? Front entrances? Side Entrances? Double entrances? Get into the stores that look like a lot of other stores.
- The outlier stores that are typical of the "problem stores" for your chain. They may be stores that are very large with low volume. (What will you do with all that space?) Small stores that have a high volume. (How can we densify the products?) The unique stores that were converted from one-of-a-kind properties and must be accounted for in every project.

- The newest stores that represent the best thinking today about what will satisfy your future shoppers. How can you adapt the good thinking and design there into retrofits for your other stores?
- The loudest stores that have managers that advocate the most when there are changes to their merchandising. Like that squeaky wheel, these managers need some attention. And let's be honest, the only reason they speak up is because they care. If you never hear from a store team, it doesn't mean they like what you send them. It may mean they don't even follow it. The stores that complain the most tend to represent many other stores that you don't ever hear from. So, get yourself to the store with the most concerns and listen to them. Chances are, you'll learn something you would have never known sitting at the keyboard.

When you visit stores, introduce yourself to store managers and aisle clerks. If required, make sure they know you are going to pay them a visit. Ask them about their perspective on how their shoppers behave in the store. Ask them what is difficult and what is easy to do when resetting planograms. Ask them for their ideas for improvements. Do NOT make commitments you cannot keep. Hear a great idea? Tell them "I like that idea. I am going to consider that." Not "Great idea – I'll make that happen." Or if you hear a complaint that you do not agree with, try to explain the reason behind the merchandising decision "I understand that your shoppers want the Italian capers, but the data suggests that keeping the pickled green beans at eye-level will be more profitable." Be prepared to hear a lot that you may not be able to control about packaging, pricing and advertising. But acknowledge them and do your best to bring their message to people who can action on it.

Bring the floorplan and make any corrections on it so that it aligns to the "real world." Ask about any discrepancies. Note any repairs or maintenance issues and pass on that information if possible. Take photos, if possible.

Watch shoppers in your categories in the stores. If possible, ask them questions when you see them searching for something or when they review many items then select one to buy. The more you can understand about what they like and dislike and how they shop, the better you will be at your job.

Set up a system for saving notes, ideas, photos and quotes that you and others can refer to in the future. IT will make a difference when you can gain a broad view of many different stores in the market.

Work a reset.

It cannot be emphasized enough. Every single planogrammer and floor planner needs to work in a store completing a reset every single year. When you work on a reset you learn so many things about the time and effort to make simple changes. You become intimately aware of the fixtures and their limitations. You build teamwork and camaraderie with the store teams. You get first-hand expertise on the products in the set. You learn about store protocols and processes and why they exist.

Honestly, I would never employ a person in space planning who did not work a reset every year. Non-negotiable.

Competitive store visits

A visit to a competitor is incredibly insightful. No matter how many times you may have been in their stores, look for what they are doing right. It is easy to look through your lens and identify what they are doing wrong. But if you look for one good idea every time you walk into a competitor's store, you can begin to understand why they have loyal shoppers.

You probably cannot take pictures, but you can watch shoppers. You can read signs. I like to measure off sections and then count assortment selection to see if I am carrying more or less products than the competition. Try to guess their CDT and merchandising goals when you review their sets. Are they highlighting their price savings? Their exclusive items? Are they too far ahead or too far behind in seasonal goods? What does their sell through look like? Do they have any operational shortcuts that make them faster?

To be a valuable partner, come to the strategic meetings with your CM with a point of view on what key competitors are doing and how. Provide any merchandising ideas you have to help the CM address gaps.

Be aware of local competitors. When you visit competitors do not just focus on the one or two national or regional players that always challenge you for shoppers. Each area is likely to have a few mom and pops or small chains that are succeeding in their market. Those are often hotbeds of innovation and risk taking where you can see something that is exceptional – but perhaps difficult to scale. Look for those ideas and think about how your company could adapt them to your store environments.

Surveys

It is common for space teams to send stores surveys to understand current conditions when beginning a new project. While ideally space systems and stores should remain synchronized so that store changes are known, a survey can help to establish the baseline when starting a project.

Surveys commonly sent to stores confirm things like:

- Overall height, width and depth of planogram sections for a category.
- Section adjacencies for the planogram.
- Length of peg hooks.
- Slatwall or pegboard spacing.
- Sign holder configurations.
- Presence of dividers, pushers or other merchandising systems.

A good practice is to ask yes/no questions on surveys so stores can respond quickly and accurately. Including pictures are also helpful so stores can understand what they are being asked to measure or evaluate.

Labor Estimates

Most retailers create a labor estimate for each planogram change. These are based on the item count in the planogram, the merchandising fixtures being changed (Peg hooks versus shelves. Do shelf heights change?), the degree of change (refresh or fully remerchandise) and the difficulty in merchandising the category. For example, it is much easier to move and remerchandise dishwasher detergent than large bags of dog food.

Those estimates are usually created each year to align to the planogram change calendar. But after the planograms have been completed, the before/after comparison should be recalibrated so that stores can get a more accurate view of the work hours that will be needed to complete the change.

Most retailers have a labor estimate worksheet that requires elements like "refresh or reset," number of sections affected, merchandising style, special sign requirements, etc. For example, a household cleaners reset for an 8' planogram would take 30 minutes for a 4' section, so 1 hour total per store. While a refresh would only take 15 minutes per 4' section so 30 minutes total. Labor estimates should be recalibrated and shared with retail operations teams so that labor hours can be properly budgeted.

The Reset Packet

The culmination of work for a space planning team is to hand off a merchandising change packet to for store teams to execute planogram changes. Depending on the nature of the work and the store labor model, the people who will conduct the change may be internal store team members, internal traveling merchandising teams or third-party labor teams hired to execute the changes in your stores. In any case, the instructions and execution details should always be provided assuming that the readers are seeing their first ever planogram change. Too many space planning team members become complacent about the materials they see every single day and presume that everyone has the same level of familiarity.

While some retailers still print and distribute planogram reset packages to their stores, most distribute planogram changes electronically and stores retrieve, sometimes print....and review their instructions in store. Typical planogram reset packages include:

- A short, written overview of the change highlighting significant changes or additions, external sign or fixtures needed to complete the change and contacts for troubleshooting.
- A single page image of the new planogram with signs in place. This gives the execution team an overall view of the final product.
- A section-by-section image of the new planogram with each section as its own page. Shelf heights are noted. This is commonly printed out and taped to the back of each section while executing the planogram
- A listing of all items being deleted so that they can be removed to a clearance location.
- A "line listing" of each product in shelf order with the proper number of facings so that execution team members can see exactly where each item belongs.

Optional elements include:

- Vendor disposition instructions if there are discontinued items that are to be returned.
- Sign or POP display instructions.
- Topline sales reports for top sellers.
- New product details – features and benefits to highlight to shoppers.
- Interim instructions if goods will not arrive in time or if there are elements that will be missing for a known period of time.
- Optional merchandising directions – if the planogram version is not

specific for the store, there might be several "acceptable" options for stores to select and adapt for their conditions. This is most common in fashion and home goods displays.

While some retailers still use paper or PDF versions of the packet, more retailers are adopting a completely digital planogram packet that is delivered to a tablet or other in-store device. One of the benefits of a digital version is that execution team members can zoom into anything for clarity. And once they have completed their work, they can immediately alert space planning that the work has been done, take photos or create a help ticket if something went wrong. Photos are especially powerful when they automatically become a part of the store's catalogue so that space planners and others can pull up the store and see its most recent documented conditions.

Planogram Mock-ups

Despite the analysis and insights that a computerized planogram system can provide, many retailers continue to rely on a planogram mock-up process. That is, a physical creation of the merchandising with product samples in a real store or a testing location as a step in their planogram approval process.

In most cases, there is a non-public location for the mockup. Vendors or DCs are instructed to send samples of every item in consideration to that location. Administratively, there is nearly always full-time headcount to operate such a location. Fixtures, signs, flooring, lighting and all merchandising elements need to be re-created in the demonstration space. The process of receiving, staging and removing product is not to be underestimated. Because there is never enough space to create every version of the planogram, mockups usually focus on the most common version, the largest and the smallest versions. Walk throughs have to be scheduled weeks or months in advance to secure all the goods and get the fixtures set properly. When there is slippage in timelines from suppliers, walkthroughs can be counterproductive.

Store prototypes and mock-up rooms should be treated as highly secure and confidential locations. People who are not employees - including fixture vendors, printers and systems vendors – may pass through and have conversations with your competition. New business ideas, new products and upcoming promotions are not public knowledge. Outside access could have a detrimental effect on competitive campaigns and even stock value, if leaked. With valuable products onsite, they become magnets for inventory losses. Since the products will never sell through, they are unsustainable environments for perishable goods with expiration dates.

The planogram mockup may or may not happen prior to computerized planogram development. In lagging organizations, vendors are invited to build the merchandising, the buyers and others review the results, tweak it and then the planogram team comes afterward to capture the results. It can be a battle over space that is unmodulated by retailer data.

In other cases, the space planning team and the buyers work together to build the prototypical set. They may review data as they create the merchandising before presenting the results to divisional VPs and other internal partners. Quite often this is formal part of the category line review and the walk-through caps weeks of work. It is the final meeting where strategies and financial outcomes can be challenged by executives. The executive sign off is a stage gate that permits all of the downstream work to begin. Like setting up new items in DC's, ordering first cases of new items, marking down clearance products and budgeting labor for the reset.

Other companies have a store prototype in a warehouse or other location that they use in a modified way for mocking up new merchandising schemes. In those cases, there is just one set for each category and the placement and adjacencies attempt to emulate an actual store. This is easier to administer since it is meant to represent one store and does not need to change over as much as a mock-up area that needs to house multiple versions of each category's planograms. The store prototype is very helpful for seeing marketing materials in a store context before committing to an expensive purchase.

Mock-up rooms and store prototypes are both excellent venues for reviewing and testing new fixture designs and finishes. It is common for category managers to want customized merchandising for their products that they think will showcase their category perfectly. But sometimes those optimized features do not fit within the context of the store's overall environment. I am thinking of the retailer who had a funky fresh-off-the-boat import shop. Their spice category managers wanted a sleek chrome and acrylic dispenser system that stuck eighteen inches into the aisle. While the fixture package worked well in keeping the small jars aligned, it went against the brand image for the rest of the store. That became glaringly obvious when the new metal system was installed in the mock-up room.

The store prototype is an excellent location for reviewing a major new product line or business extension before unveiling it to the public. Even with a robust testing or piloting process, setting up a major new business line in a prototype store can help identify merchandising gaps before going onto the market. A store prototype can help when reviewing business adjacencies and fixture compatibility. Look for alignment issues with shelf heights, continuity issues and unnatural shopping patterns. If the new merchandising requires demonstration models or power, be sure to test them hundreds of times in the controlled prototype room to prevent failure in the field.

The other way that a mock-up room or a store prototype can be valuable is in creating store directions and communications. Capture merchandising changes and directions in short videos that go to your stores for review on demand rather than writing up long-form directions. Especially when setting up critical elements like holiday display pieces or seasonal signs and fixtures. Using the physical space to talk through a merchandising conversion can be time saving for both the internal team who has to produce the instructions and the store teams who can simply watch and recreate the effort in their store.

Finally, we cannot depart from this topic without talking about housekeeping. The downfall of nearly all on premise store environments is the care and maintenance of the space. Samples are discarded in piles and pallets that do not get disposed of properly. The best practice is to set up a schedule with a nearby charity who will claim all goods once the planograms are struck. The space needs to be included in regular store maintenance schedules to ensure that it represents the same conditions as the stores in the market. Ship seasonal signs and promotional packages to the prototype and see that they are both set up and removed on time. Keep excess fixtures organized. If you are a vendor who is lucky enough to be included in the space, make sure that you only leave with the products you look after. Be fair and honest. Being the last one to walk the set does not mean you are the last one to adjust facings and placements. Help out more than you need to, and you will be trusted in the future.

Technology - Mastering The Systems

L ike other retail disciplines, there are a variety of software solutions that your company may employ to produce its store space plans. And while there are many different solution providers, they all basically require the same things: accurate store layouts, detailed product information, and reliable up-to-date performance data. There is a detailed discussion of the item and store attribute data in the companion book *The Space Planner's Handbook* by Flora Delaney. But for now, let's take a broader view of the space and space-adjacent merchandising systems needed to deliver a unified shopper experience in stores today.

What It Takes to Succeed

As with all other systems, the data integrity of a space system is directly tied to the usefulness of the output. Here then are common system inputs that a space system requires and the risks to the output if they are mishandled.

Accurate and Current Layouts

Savvy retailers rely on floorplans to accurately account for fixture placement, business and planogram locations in a store, promotional locations, shopper experience and host of other outcomes. Naturally, the floorplans must be accurate and current. Supply chain teams rely on floor plans to understand seasonal and promotional inventory allocations and each store's holding capacity for those high-volume allocations. Store execution partners, rely on floor plans as an accurate repository for every type of fixture and their location in the store. Which is critical when new fixtures need to be delivered to a store to support new programs. For marketing partners, floorplans are a source for directing temporary sign allocations and promotional space availability. For analytic partners, floorplans are the foundation for space productivity metrics which identify businesses that deserve more or less space in upcoming remodel efforts. For store operators, the floorplans ensure that programs, planograms, inventory, and signs that are delivered to the store have a home.

Floorplans are the foundation for planograms. If a floorplan is not accurate, the planograms assigned to the store may not be accurate. Which means products and programs can be sent to the store that will not be merchandised properly. When the program or products do not meet sales forecasts, the entire company will be left to wonder if the reason was a poorly constructed program or if it just never got a chance because the stores could not execute it as designed. At a strategic level, it means that the company cannot test, learn and adapt to build more success. Since it can never know the root cause of when it does not fully succeed.

For this reason, the floorplanning system must have a regular cadence of producing floorplans that stay updated to reflect the conditions in the stores. Store leadership need to support those plans and hold themselves accountable for updating the floorplans when there are changes that are initiated in the stores. Ideally, those changes are communicated and approved with enough time that the floorplans stay synchronized and products flow smoothly to their locations in every store.

Past methods for capturing floorplans included store surveys, third-party inspectors, floorplan "red line" processes with operations teams and other manual efforts. Those processes have inherent "lag" which means that the stores are rarely up to date in the corporate system. To reduce that lag, new technologies like robots with image recognition (IR) software or three-dimensional cameras are deployed in stores to capture real-time changes to the store conditions. Retailers are embedding cameras and IR devices in ceilings or atop tall gondolas to record both store conditions as well as shopper interactions. Some technologies claim to capture a digital twin of every store in their fleet in real time which creates a continuously updated real-time store environment for every store in their space systems.

Currently, most floorplanning teams are resourced to keep pace with new store openings and regularly scheduled store remodels or relocations. But when major renovation initiatives cause major changes across the entire chain, the team can be stretched beyond its capacity. For many retailers, the solution is to turn to outside resources during peak production periods.

Contractors can be a source for extra capacity if your team can clearly define the criteria they need to change as they edit the store files. Contractors can be hired for full-time staff augmentation and your team can triple or quadruple its size overnight. To succeed, have a clear plan for onboarding contractors, providing clear direction, monitoring their work and management capacity for oversight. A benefit of the contractor model is that strong performers can become a hiring funnel into your organization as floor planning roles open. A drawback to the contractor model is that you may have to interview many candidates before you find the right talent to augment your staff. You will also have to supply their technology to complete the job.

Outsourcing to third party providers is another way to cover production peaks. Signing a contract with a company that specializes in helping retailers with their merchandising staffing is a way to have a more turn-key solution when you need additional staffing. You will still have to create solid criteria and project definitions, but you are likely to work with a more experienced team that will be familiar with your stores and not need the same level of onboarding. Third party providers will typically perform to a service level agreement that is mutually defined. You may have less control over which people work on your project. However, third party suppliers manage time tracking, provide the technology and typically have an efficient process for producing results.

Between those solutions is the contracted overseas staffing model. Many retailers have a fully dedicated team that operates in other countries to provide both a lower-cost production team as well as round-the-clock productivity. Handing off work from time zone to time zone can reduce the overall duration of long timelines. But it requires tight management, clear communication and integrated systems to be as seamless as possible.

If you find that your organization has outdated floorplans and you cannot rely on the plans in your system, it is time to assess the resources you can gather to address your situation. With a small chain, you may be able to produce updated floorplans with internal resources. Can your team travel to enough locations over the course of a year to measure and update the store floorplans? If not, can you teach the people who regularly visit the stores how to update (redline) the floorplans to provide updated layouts? Can you count on division managers or even store managers to accurately read their current floorplan and update it? With focus, training and strong partnership, I have seen chains up to 1000+ stores use only their internal teams to produce accurate floorplans in under a year.

If you do not have access to internal resources, there are outside firms that provide this service. Companies can deploy teams of people across the country and deliver updated floorplans in weeks – not months. Depending on the partner you select, they can also validate exterior elevations, backroom conditions, capture planograms, and update the floorplans.

Be very careful about defining what your company truly needs with that investment. Can you make use of digital twin store details that provide 3-D renderings of every shelf, peg, sign and light fixture in a store? Before being seduced by the visual beauty of what some VR companies can produce, make sure that you can take advantage of the information and its granularity. If you are considering a solution that goes beyond the standard information you currently use in executing assortment transitions, investigate needs from other teams like marketing, in-store media or shopper research. You may find that their benefits can justify an investment into a VR store environment.

While producing updated floorplans for the store fleet, you must also initiate the resourcing and processes for maintaining them. More than one retailer has spent millions to create updated floorplans only to have them age beyond usefulness in a few years. You will need to have the resources to keep pace with changes, the process for initiating changes and a communication channel that validates execution or changes made in the field that need to be noted on floorplans. But perhaps more challenging, you will need to have cross-functional buy-in and accountability to make floorplan accuracy non-negotiable. Senior executive commitment in this area is the #1 indicator of success.

The Physical Laws of Fixtures

With floorplans resolved, the next critical system component is the fixture library. Tremendous operational value and cost savings are unlocked when the space planning system's fixture library is accurate and complete. In this context, we are considering fixtures as both the macro fixtures that construction teams build that become a store's framework to the micro fixtures where products are merchandised.

Space systems typically include a set of fixture templates that can be repurposed by users to create basic types of fixtures. Gondolas, back boards, kickplates, endcaps, pinwheels, H-Fixtures, nested tables and apparel hanging rounders are common macro fixture types that are placed on floorplans. Shelves, bins, baskets, pegboards, slatwall, rods, bars and peg hooks are micro fixtures that you may find in a prepopulated micro space solution. Let's be clear: *these are not your fixtures.* They are examples of the fixture types and the physical laws that your fixtures are patterned after. These fixture templates that are included in most space planning systems are merely the containers for the physical rules about how those fixture types behave. For example, peg hooks are only able to be merchandised with products dangling below them. Hanging bars must anchor into solid uprights to hold the weight of hanging apparel.

Mature space practitioners use those fixture templates as the basis for creating a unique fixture package. A retailer's fixture package includes the exact make, model, color, finish and supplier for every element in the store. Properly done, they use the fixture manufacturer's "cut sheet" to capture the precise specifications for each element. Thus, when a store project needs to source the fixtures, all of the details are available through the space system's bill of materials.

Taken to an extreme, add and store details in the fixture dataset like embedded videos that show how to build the fixtures as part of their details. If possible, allow vendors access to the fixture library and arrange for them to be responsible for keeping the pricing and availability up to date. Much like a retailer has a vendor portal to allow suppliers to enter new item details, give your fixture (and sign) vendors access to a portal so they keep your fixtures up to date.

Products and their Images

For every product that will be planogrammed, the product data set must be available to the space planning system. Besides the obvious data elements like name, UPC and merchandising hierarchy classifications, there are several other key data elements that ought to be part of any product library. These data elements ought to be ingested from the system of record for products within a retailer. Sometimes referred to as the SKU Master, it is a database that catalogues all relevant static information about the product. Here is a way to think about those elements:

Where and how the data is accessed, will vary depending on your particular implementation. SAAS, cloud-based systems tend to use APIs that keep the data continuously refreshed. While on-premises, databased systems tend to use batch file integrations on a refresh schedule. There are a few things to watch out for depending on your setup.

Caution #1: Space-only attributes and where they are housed. For most other merchandising systems (pricing, assortment, promotion) there are common needs for the data elements that are in the Customer-facing, Inventory and Performance attributes. Those data elements are more likely to be captured in enterprise data governance practices and properly cleansed and updated. But the Merchandising attributes are likely to be hosted within the space planning system alone. Which means that space planning needs its own processes and governance to keep that data clean and accurate. Many larger space teams have a "librarian" role to update and cleanse merchandising data for the shared space team. In more rogue organizations, every user is able to enter the data they require for their project. Which is where errors and omissions can cause issues.

For example, let's take "crush." That is the data element that describes the degree to which a package can be reduced (crushed) on shelf when it is merchandised. Think of bags of chips or cotton balls. If there is no master control over "crush" a less-than-scrupulous planogrammer can add crush to any item that does not fit on a shelf. A quick review of the "crush" data element combined with the package type of each product can quickly identify where users have allowed cans, bottles and cartons to be crushed. Which may make for an attractive planogram on screen but caused hundreds or thousands of stores to make corrections while the planogram was being set.

Caution #2: Once the "back door" access of creating data elements in a local space system exists, it doesn't take long for a compliant space planning team to create fake products or place holders for new items that are planned for an upcoming assortment transition. Place holders are meant to stand in for items that will be available when the reset occurs, but which are not quite set up properly in the retailer's system. Maybe the final package specifications are not settled with a private brand producer. Maybe there are still negotiations amongst several suppliers and the ultimate selection is yet to be made. Maybe the product is an exclusive item, and its case pack and pricing are not complete. In any case, a frantic buyer may ask a space planner to "dummy up" an item so that there is a spot on the planogram for the product. But if the planogram publishes with the placeholder item still on the set, several unintended downstream actions can occur:

1. The product may never be properly set up or purchased. So now that space on the POG must be reallocated and a new POG must be re-published to the stores.
2. The product may remain on the set and reflect wrong information. Like a dummy UPC 0000000001 which causes inventory allocations and batch price tag jobs to fail.
3. The placeholder product may never be properly replaced with the actual product leading to item proliferation in the product database and ultimately causing a lack of confidence in space system data integrity.

In any case, the use of placeholder products is a common practice which regularly causes problems for retailers and their stores. To avoid this situation, consider either requiring items that are properly set up in the enterprise system of record permission to be placed on planograms or have a data validation step which strips placeholders out of planograms before they are published.

Product images are a separate data set and usually held in another location that is separate from a product's attribute data. Product images are discussed in detail in *The Space Planner's Guidebook (also by the author)*. But let's review product images from a system point of view.

Image specifications generally follow GS1 guidelines[6] which creates stan-dards and uniformity for companies to share their digital assets. Space planning image capture teams are advised to follow those standards to ensure that their system properly uses images since space systems adhere to those standards. But for most companies, the need for digital images extends far beyond space. Too often unconnected image libraries exist in multiple locations throughout an organization. Image libraries may exist for marketing, e-commerce, packaging, marketing research, space planning, inventory planning and more.

To efficiently manage diverse audiences, a DAM (Digital Asset Management) system is one of the best ways to ensure that images are up to date and accessible to all teams. Because it is one centralized location, it is easier for users (and systems) to access the most up to date files and components as well as reducing redundancy across the enterprise. Companies can implement security controls so that images are not inadvertently overwritten, intentionally appropriated or published while still in development. Brand redesigns and re-packaging efforts can be secured until they are released for consumption. Marketing, e-commerce and brand teams can collaborate on selecting the proper shots to be used across the enterprise. Space planning is one of many consumers of the DAM images. But a DAM can eliminate replicating thousands or millions of image files in a space-only image library.

---

[6] GS1 has a product image specification standard that establishes rules for the storage of digital images associated to products and provides details on all aspects of digital image storing which was ratified by retail and producer representatives in Feb 2019 which is available online.

How systems fit together

A space system is just one of the critical merchandising systems that a retailer must have to operate efficiently. At the highest level there are families of systems that a retailing company requires to operate:

- **Supplier systems** – Vendor management, Import/Domestic Sourcing, Pricing & Terms Quotations, Order processing, PO Management, Demand Planning by vendor, Sales and Inventory Receipt Management. Ties to Accounts Payable systems and the General Ledger.
- **Customer Systems** – Customer profiling & segmenting, Loyalty programs, Relationship Management, Market Research
- **Labor management** – Scheduling, Timekeeping, etc. Ties to HR systems, Payroll systems and the General Ledger.
- **Logistics/Supply Chain Systems** – Financial Planning, Warehouse and Transportation Management. Inventory Optimization and Monitoring. E-commerce fulfillment.
- **Channel Transactional Systems** – Website customer care, shopping, click analyses, and e-commerce order management. Brick and mortar POS systems, perpetual inventory, Store receiving, Price ticketing and signage, DSD/Store receiving.
- **Merchandising Systems** – Planning: Assortment Planning, Open-to-buy, Forecasting, Promotion Management, Pricing Management, Markdown Management, Merchandise Planning, Space Planning
- **Reporting and Analytics Systems** - Data Warehousing and Business Intelligence, Machine Learning, AI.

Each company will configure their system architecture differently. Some will leverage an ERP (Enterprise Resource Planning) system that essentially manages every aspect of their business. The fully architected solution comes pre-built with the integrations and shared data layers fully embedded in the suite. An ERP, however, can only be minimally customized which means that a retailer will have to adopt the ERP's processes to use it. For example, if the ERP is built such that only items that are already set up in the item management module are available to be included in the promotional planning module, it means that items that are currently being sourced overseas for holidays but are not yet set up cannot be added to the Black Friday ad plan. There are dozens of examples of where a system's constrictions regulate how a retailer can operate when they select an "off the shelf" ERP solution.

Nevertheless, ERPs have tremendous power to harmonize cross-department practices and provide insights that leverage data that exists in many different functional areas. ERPs promote their ability to have "one version of the truth" because data is consistent and constant in every operational module. When there are multiple systems operating within a company, it is common to have discrepancies and confusion because of conflicting information existing in different systems. It can be as elemental as different systems calculating Gross or Net profit differently! For companies who want to align on a standard operating model and cut the total cost of ownership for licensing and maintaining many different systems, ERPs are a good idea.

Other companies will leverage a different architecture strategy and seek out point solutions or "best of breed" solutions for each area separately and then integrate them where necessary to share data. This strategy maximizes flexibility and customization so that each functional system is tailored to meet the exact requirements for the business. Upgrading components is less disruptive to the entire organization so the company can continually monitor the solution landscape and select more appealing solutions when they enter the market.

It is highly unusual for an ERP to include an effective space planning module in their suite of solutions. Which is why most companies have a stand-alone space planning tool. Or several.

Finally, there is another option that some companies leverage in their system architecture: building their own software. Building software from the ground up is expensive. It requires development resources, hardware and software expertise and ongoing maintenance and upgrades that are completely shouldered by the company. Unlike a licensed software solution where the costs are shared across many companies using the same solution. (with profits returning to the software provider, naturally.)

A Note on The Strategy of Building Software:

Building and maintaining a proprietary solution only makes sense for a company if the solution that they build will provide a marked competitive advantage over any other solution in the market. For example, if a fast fashion retailer captured market advantage and sales through its unbeatable design to production to sales floor speed, a proprietary solution where sales forecasts along with product design and sourcing optimization occurred within the same system would help it maintain a competitive advantage over other companies that were using best of breed solutions in each of those areas. In that situation, the company would be respected for investing in creating its own custom solution.

But for Space Planning, floor layout and planogram production, there is little advantage for a retailer or their supplier to build their own solution. Far more common is for a retailer to create custom solutions or integrations that surround a best of breed space planning solution. There are many who have built their own reporting and analytics for space. Or they have created a unique store-facing portal that includes space plans within it. Some have a proprietary assortment planning solution that is "space aware" and supports a round-trip journey of data from planogram to assortment plan and back to planogram.

Whether a company selects an ERP, a best of breed, a custom software strategy, or a combination of them all, it is helpful to see how systems fit together. A system map is in the Appendix for your reference. Each company will create their unique system map but reviewing it will help you see how data elements are shared and how systems fit together.

Critical Integrations for Space Systems

When a space system is installed, there are integrations to other systems. Some companies choose to only include a few. Others will create a fully integrated technology ecosystem. But these are the most common:

1. Space imports data from a product master. (Space rarely exports to a product master.)
2. Space imports product images from a digital asset repository. (Space rarely exports to a digital "library" or DAM.)
3. Space imports data from a store master. (Space infrequently exports to a store master.)
4. Space imports performance data from a POS system. (Space never exports to POS data.)
5. Space exports the planogram to store assignment data to a central repository for reporting or to an inventory allocation and replenishment system.
6. Space exports a shelf capacity by planogram (and, thus, by store) which may include a minimum, maximum and target shelf stock to an inventory allocation and replenishment system.
7. Space exports position data by shelf type to a price tag batch printing file so that the correct price tag types are printed in the same order as the product is merchandised by POG.
8. Space exports the planogram, line listing, and other execution instructions for stores as PDFs for store retrieval or to a store-facing operational system.
9. Space exports store-specific promotional locations by store to a promotional planning system. Space may also export promotional sign

specifications by store location to a promotional planning system. Space imports offer by store location promotional plans from a promotional planning system to merchandise those promotional planogram changes.

10. Space exports fixture bill of materials by store to a procurement team to fulfill fixture orders to support a new store, remodel or major planogram change.

11. Space exports pre-selected data elements to a reporting database to provide company-wide access to space analysis. Space allocation rollups at the brand, category, department levels are most common. Less commonly, there is a duplicate reporting database that replicates the space production database.

The Space System as Foundational Data

The space system is ideal to be a source of record for the fixtures that are in each store. For the sign packages that are in every store. For the space that is available for each category within each store.

But if you wish to extend space data to more of the enterprise, there is one key caveat for using space data more universally: *what percent of the items sold in a store are on a planogram?*

If there were 100% of all the items sold in each store on a planogram, then the space system would be an ideal source for accounting for where every single item in the retail system is authorized for sale. If there were an item to POG to store relationship, the item is authorized for the store.

However, if local store managers or merchandisers are allowed to order products for their store(s) on their own, then the planogram is no longer a comprehensive list of items authorized for a store. Only the POS system would be accurate (if the local team set up the items properly in the POS system.)

If promotional teams or seasonal teams are allowed to send products to stores for temporary displays without a planogram, then the space system is no longer an accurate system of record.

If DSD vendors are allowed to have control over their "doors" or placement when they replenish and merchandise products in the stores, then the space system is not an accurate system of record.

All of these situations are very common. Leaving planogram-to-store data as the starting point for understanding which items sell in each store. But it must be augmented with auxiliary reporting from the POS system or the promotional system or other data sources to get a complete picture of reality.

That matters when a company tries to conduct a space productivity analysis at the category level and uses category sales compared to planogrammed space. Let's say that a market had a very strong potato chip vendor who delivered DSD. All the stores in that market leveraged the vendor who regularly stacks cases of locally made potato chips in the vestibule of the stores. An analysis of the stores in that market may indicate that potato chips overperform on a sales per square foot basis and that the adjacent businesses (jerky and tortilla chips) should surrender space to expand potato chips in those stores. A new planogram is issued, but it may still not include items from the local DSD vendor. All that happened is that the jerky and tortilla chip businesses were reduced, and the overall sales may not have changed for potato chips at all. In the end, inventory turn for the planogrammed chips slowed and the store went through an unnecessary disruption that did not improve its performance.

Thus, for space systems to be the source of record for other downstream systems and processes, it is important that the assortments and sales in the stores are completely accounted for in the planograms. Most retailers have pockets of clean and dirty data within space. Or it is clean up to a certain hierarchy level.

For example, a mass merchant may have completely planogrammed the center of the store. So that it can specifically know the space productivity and contribution for every *item* in the Laundry aisle. But it only knows that 2,000 square feet of space is dedicated to boys clothing. The space system does not know which fixtures had shirts or pajamas or pants. Which means that the data for boys clothing is only accurate at a *category* level. This is common for areas that have an accurate space allocation on the floor plan of a store but do not have accurate planograms. This condition typically exists for produce, meat, seafood, floral, bakery, nursery stock, lumber, and home furnishings.

Thinking about planogrammed data, however, there are some key data elements that only exist in a planogram or floor plan that other systems can use.

1. Minimum shelf presentation quantity - A calculation in the space system for number of customer facings (including stacked or nested items) times the minimum units per facing allowed in the store. Critical for new item allocations to stores.
2. Maximum shelf holding capacity - The maximum number of units that can fit on the shelf in the merchandising constraints of that particular fixture/store set. Critical for replenishment teams in setting up item order triggers and minimum order quantities.
3. Item location - The specific aisle, segment and shelf location for every planogrammed item in the store. Critical for returned merchandising, e-commerce order fulfillment from stores, shelf stocking and customer-facing shopping apps.
4. Item positional order by shelf - The exact location on a shelf each item is to one another. Critical for printing shelf price tags (permanent and promotional) in an order that is easy to execute for store team members.
5. Number of specific fixture elements required to build a section - The

exact bill of materials to execute any planogrammed section of the store. Critical for store merchandising operations to gather their materials before a new store set up, remodel or planogram change. Critical for fixture ordering teams. Critical for financial planners who must estimate the costs for remodels, new stores or other large project initiatives.

6. Items discontinued at the store level, but not the chain - The list of items that will continue to be replenished, but at fewer stores is key to building future sales forecasts by DC and vendor. Also initiates clearance price markdowns at some stores while maintaining ongoing pricing at other stores.

7. Promotional locations and their holding capacities - The total number of end caps, aisle bulk stacks, value sections, floor stands, check lane sections and any other promotional location available by store. Ideally, the cubic space available can be leveraged to right size the inventory sent to each store so that it fits into each location. Critical for promotional planning so that stores are shipped the proper promotional or seasonal inventory for each offer. Can also drive the promotional sign production when a promotion will be executed in different locations in different stores.

8. Refrigerated and frozen model management - Each store's specific appliance model tracked and monitored so that maintenance, upgrades and recalls can be targeted and managed. Critical for store operations and maintenance.

9. Fixture costs and tracking by store - the total investment into fixtures, appliances, permanent displays, etc. that are depreciated over time by site location. Critical for accounting and insurance.

Depending on the company's installation and accountability, there is much more which can be added to a space system so that there is a robust system of record for several other key elements. Here are specific examples I have seen:

1. Landlord name and leasing terms by store - housing the data in a space system instead of a real estate system allows for deeper analysis by landlord when evaluating store productivity. Also allows for direct understanding of a landlord's percentage of sales by department. Especially important in mall-based retailers where landlord negotiations are for multiple sites at once. Retailers can come to the table better understanding if a specific retailer is more critical to fine jewelry and designer wear over costume jewelry and activewear which may have much different margins.

2. Utility provider by store - critical when a store's assortment uses different levels of energy or has different internet needs than other stores. Puts a retailer in a better position to create direct product profitability metrics and negotiate different deals with utilities. Also important if the retailer is pursuing a sustainability/green energy initiative for reporting purposes.

3. Parking spaces by store - Important for measuring and planning for new stores.

4. Common Area Maintenance Fees by store - A landlord fee to cover HVAC, landscaping, maintenance, marketing and other fees for a shopping center. Critical for store contribution reporting.

5. Delivery cadence by category - when a store's delivery cadence by category (1 per week, 3 times per week, etc.) is included in planogramming, the shelf holding capacity can be aligned to the deliveries so that the inventory in the store turns at a specified goal rate. Since stores have different delivery schedules and different costs to serve, this is key to making the end-to-end supply chain as efficient as possible.

The Space System Conversion

At some point in a long space planning career, you may find yourself in a company that is converting from one space planning system to another. Changes in requirements, new advancements and changes in IT strategy can all launch a change to the space system in a company. The endeavor is not to be taken lightly. It will take time. And money. And a great deal of dedication across the organization to make the conversion. But for companies that do it right, they can leapfrog their past limits and produce more planograms more quickly and accurately than ever before.

A space planning conversion allows a company to review how it supports merchandising through processes, systems and reporting and make improvements while implementing a new system. Frankly, space planning leaders need to seize this critical moment when space planning is a priority and make as many desired changes as possible. Because as soon as the new space planning system is in run state, it will be difficult to get the resources necessary to make continuous improvements.

If your company is considering a space planning conversion, here is what you need to review and consider to ensure you are considering all of the elements that should be reviewed for enhancement.

Preparation for Core Space Systems

Compile the comprehensive details for every fixture in the stores to build a complete fixture library

- Work with new solution provider to determine which resources will build the actual fixture files (internal, implementation team, 3rd party.)
- Review, confirm, prepare fixture library for macro fixtures prior to AutoCAD file conversions into new solution provider.
- Review, confirm, prepare fixture library for micro fixtures prior to old planogram system conversions into new system.
- Build a complete peg library prior to old planogram system conversions into new system.
- Build a complete sign holder library as fixture elements for now planogram system.

Compile the required data elements for every "go forward" product to build a complete product library.

- Extract and remove old/non-replenished items from the library.
- Review remaining library data elements for accuracy.
- Correct/complete all required data elements for the product library prior to POG transition to new planogram system.

Review the entire image library for the products in the "go forward" product library.

- Flag all items that are not to standard.
- Re-capture images so that all products in the image library are to standard.
- Evaluate the current storage location for the current product library and evaluate its potential for future needs.

Create a go forward process for ensuring accurate and complete data & image capture for new items.

- Review current process and operations.
- Build new process and operations with RACI and timeline.
- Acquire any necessary tools for data and image capture.
- For example: calipers, digital camera, lightbox, Photoshop®, digital scale.

Review all current space data integrations.

- Document all current space data integrations (import & export) including system sources, timing, format and data elements for turnover during new system implementation.

Review all current space reporting or future reporting needs.

- Document all current known uses of space data elements in reporting within the entire company.
- Workshop possible future space reporting need with relevant teams including merchants, inventory, store operations, finance.
- Document the future space reporting "wish list" for exploration during the new system implementation.

Identify the correct and complete floor plan (usually AutoCAD) files that will be transitioned into the new floor planning system.

- Ensure every store has a complete and accurate floor plan/AutoCAD file.
- Ensure that every store has standardized naming for fixtures, departments, obstructions, planograms/categories, etc. for the merchandising layer of the floorplan.
- Ensure that every store file has a consistent naming convention.
- Consider how current and future floorplan files will be tagged for conversion to maintain data integrity.
- Determine whether any old floorplan files are needed for conversion into the new floor planning system for historical record or if they can be archived.

Identify the correct and complete planogram files that will be transitioned into the new planogram system.

- Ensure every category has a complete and accurate floor plan placement.
- Ensure that every planogram has standardized naming for current fixtures.
- Flag planograms that will need post-conversion processing to add incremental items such as sign holders or other elements.
- Ensure that every planogram file has a consistent naming convention.
- Ensure that planogram to store mappings can be accurately identified using current system reporting or records.
- Consider how current and future planogram files will be tagged for

conversion to maintain data integrity.
- Determine whether any old planogram files are needed for conversion into the new planogramming system for historical record or if they can be archived.

Preparation with possible Cross-Functional Process Improvements

- Review current store labor allocation methods and how it could be refined/improved with more POG granularity for stores.
- Consider how labor might be more precisely budgeted with insights into planogram size and scope.
- Define and develop a proposal for testing/refinement/adoption that would better match planogram changes with the labor to conduct the changes for the store.
- Review current Sign directions to stores and how/if they need to be represented in planograms
- If signs are to be included, determine how sign identifiers can match an image library.
- Confirm future process and procedures with all sign partners including print files sent to printers.
- Include sign integrations as part of space planning implementation scope.
- Prepare a plan for testing sign integrations (if necessary) in the new space planning system.

Review Promotional support by space planning and the processes for space planning support for promotional locations and merchandising.

- Document current promotional processes and space planning materials.
- Capture requirements from store operations and promotional planning to understand and optimize promotional execution.
- Document a new future process, if efficiencies are identified.

- Test and adjust future process, if necessary.
- Include future promotional process as part of space planning implementation scope.

Review closeout and clearance processes.

- Document current closeout/clearance process and the transition plan for end-of-life items.
- Capture requirements from store operations and replenishment to understand and optimize planogram support for end-of-life products.
- Document a new future process, if necessary.
- Test and adjust future process, if necessary.
- Communicate and train any changes necessary to support new support for merchandising end-of-life products.

Review new store opening process.

- Space Team reviews for possible changes that a new space planning system implementation will require.
- If necessary, convene a cross-functional team that supports new store openings and review adjustments to timelines, integrations and communications so that a new space planning implementation will meet or exceed current new store opening standards.
- Include future new store opening process as part of space planning implementation scope.

Review store remodeling process

- Space Team reviews for possible changes that a new space planning system implementation will require.
- If necessary, convene a cross-functional team that supports store remodeling and review adjustments to timelines, integrations and communications so that a new space planning implementation will meet

or exceed current store remodeling standards.

- Include future store remodeling process as part of space planning implementation scope.

Review store relocation process.

- Space Team reviews for possible changes that a Relex implementation will require.
- If necessary, convene the cross-functional team that supports store relocations and review adjustments to timelines, integrations and communications so that a Relex implementation will meet or exceed current NSO standards.
- Include future store relocation process as part of space planning implementation scope.

Review GNFR (Goods Not For Resale[7]) support from Space Planning.

- If planogram or space planning resources are used to initiate GNFR allocations to stores, document how that is done today.
- Determine if GNFR processes would be improved with any space support.
- If so, document and test a future plan for GNFR support and operations.
- Include GNFR requirements as part of space planning implementation scope.
- If not, eliminate GNFR from any space planning implementation scope.

Review/recommend a planogram lifecycle (see Figure 19.)

---

[7] Goods Not For Resale include items necessary for operating a store which may be allocated to a new store prior to opening (such as mops, buckets, ladders, price guns, name tags, white boards, clipboards, etc.) and items that are replenished once a store is open (such as register tape rolls, cleaning supplies, light bulbs, etc.) Those elements may or may not be accounted for in a space planning system to allow a retailer to use their normal internal allocation and replenishment systems to support the stores.

- Review current planogram lifecycle stages and stage gates.
- For example: work in process, approved, communicated, LIVE, historical, archived.
- Confirm or change for new space planning system implementation.

Review/recommend a floorplan lifecycle.

- Review current floorplan lifecycle stages and stage gates.
- For example: work in process, proposed, approved, communicated, LIVE, historical, archived.
- Confirm or change for new space planning system implementation

Review current store planogram instruction packages and how they could be refined/improved with more specificity to support efficiencies for stores.

- Consider how instruction packets might be more precisely communicated to allow stores to meet or exceed their current planogram compliance but with more focused instructions.
- Consider how to categorize planogram changes to trigger the proper instruction details for the stores (single item swaps versus entire planogram remerchandising or planogram change with/without fixture changes, for example.)
- Identify the components of a planogram instruction packet that could be automated or eliminated to make production more accurate and efficient.
- Confirm current section numbering, naming.
- Confirm current shelf numbering, naming.
- Confirm current product position numbering, naming.
- Review future state technology solutions and whether to adopt them or use the new planogram system's native instructions.
- Define and develop a proposal for testing/refinement/adoption that would better match planogram instructions with the planogram scope of change.
- Create output templates for each planogram "type" category.

- Turnover planogram output requirements as part of space planning implementation scope.

Assortment Planning and Dual Location Placement.

- Review and document the current process for allocating items to store locations.
- Consider planogram variations that might meet store space constraints more effectively.
- Consider how item rationalization may have to be considered in small stores.
- Convene a cross-functional team to review current assortment planning and dual location or combination planogram placements and possible future changes.
- If necessary, pursue a change to current practices around assortment planning and dual location and combination planogram placements.

Conversion and Implementation – Technical Implementation

Determine whether the entire implementation can be completed with your internal technical resources and an implementation team from the new space pollution provider or if you will need to use a technical implementation services provider.

- Review the new space solution provider's preferred technical partners against your own internal specifications.
- If using a third-party technical implementation partner, determine if you will contract with them separately or if they will subcontract to the new space systems team.

With the new space planning solution provider, define an integration approach and system landscape for data exchange as well as test vs production environments.

- Review and approve standardized interface specifications and communications/timelines.
- Provide and receive sample files (format configurations) for all expected data exchange files.
- Test with subset sample files.

Stage and turnover fixture library – including pegs and sign holders – to the new space planning solution provider.

- Validate that fixture behave as expected in 3D environment.

Stage and turnover product library to the new space planning solution provider.

- Validate that products behave as expected in 3D environment.

Stage and turnover store master data to the new space panning solution provider.

Configure the new planogram system to integrate with image library.

- Validate that images render as expected in 3D environment.

Configure the new planogram system to integrate with sign library

Configure the new planogram system to integrate with store performance (POS) files.

- Configure the new space planning system to receive historical and daily data files.

- Complete data integration testing and validation with "round trip" data accuracy.
- Test outbound system integrations to store price printing file, inventory allocation (shelf capacity) file and any others.

Floorplan/AutoCAD file conversion.

- floorplan migration rehearsal and configurations with data mapping.
- Turnover all store AutoCAD files for floor plan conversion.
- Post-conversion cleanup.

Planogram file conversion.

- Planogram migration rehearsal and configurations with data mapping
- Turnover all previous planogram files for planogram conversion
- Post-conversion cleanup

(The assumption all of this is done in a test environment before migrating to a production environment.)

Conversion and Implementation – Business Configurations

- Define and manage user access and permissions.
- Document process for new hires.
- Document process for non-space planning additions.
- Communicate process changes.

Floor plan Implementation.

- Define and add floor plan lifecycles.
- Test and validate.
- Define and build in-system reporting.
- Test and validate.

- Post-Conversion business acceptance testing.
- Fixture validation.
- Departmental zone.
- POG to store assignment validation.
- Space metric validation.

Planogram Implementation.

- Define and add planogram Lifecycles.
- Test and validate.
- Define and build in-system reporting.
- Test and validate.
- Define and build output templates.
- Test and validate.
- Define and build any non-standard product labels in the new planogram system.
- Test and validate.
- Define and build any non-standard highlights in the new planogram system.
- Test and validate.
- Define and build planogram repository folder structure.
- Test and validate.
- Complete post-conversion business acceptance testing.
- Fixture validation.
- Product position validation.
- Space metric validation.
- Sign integration validation.

Automation development.

- Review standard automations available in the new planogram system and select most valuable modules for your organization.
- Test planogram automations to build custom scripts/work packages and

output
- Refine scripts/work packages.
- Test and validate.
- Document automation expectations for planogram team.

Implementation – Training & Communication

For space planning users

- Identify subject matter experts/super users & responsibilities in training.
- Review all standard training modules for the new space planning system.
- Customize training elements that need changes/refinements for your implementation.
- Create training program for current space planning team members – including automations.
- Create/identify training program for new hires.
- Execute space planning training.

For non-space planning users

- Review any changes that non-space planning team members will have to accommodate with the new space planning implementation.
- Consider changes to:
- Data elements and reporting
- Instruction packets to stores
- Promotional placements and instructions to stores
- Store price tag issue escalation
- Store planogram issue escalation
- Store floorplan issue escalation

FLOOR PLANNING SYSTEM GO LIVE

PLANOGRAM SYSTEM GO LIVE

Ongoing Support and Continuous Improvement (Sustain)

Technical Support.

- Create a shared definition for issue escalation path with the new space solution provider for technical support.
- Handover ongoing technical support to proper IT help desk for Level 1-XX support.
- Sunset old space planning system and all data integrations that solely support the old space planning system.

Business Support.

- Create a shared definition for issue escalation path with the new space solution provider for business support.
- Handover ongoing business support to proper internal super user/admin.
- Create a standing business rhythm with the new space solution provider for ongoing business dialogue.

Final Wrap up session with the implementation team.

CELEBRATE!

Analyzing – Mastering The Science

While it is true that space planning is key to attractive, well-operating stores, space planners succeed when they approach their work understanding that the function is data driven. They create merchandising plans that integrate, transform and produce data that other systems require. The data within space plans is amongst the richest of the entire retail operation. It contains the sales, placement, inventory and shopper decisions made at the moment of decision. Too many space operators fail to share the insights that are available with the buyers, inventory managers and store teams that could take critical action with that knowledge. Unlocking the data of space planning promotes cross-functional alignment and insights across the entire enterprise. So, in this chapter, let's talk about the basic building blocks for creating space planning insights.

Planogram Analysis - The Single Planogram

Let's start with a planogrammer who wishes to analyze one single planogram. Let us also suppose that it is a planogram that is active and executed in 50 stores. With the proper data integrations to the planogramming software, the sales performance, retail prices and costs for some historical period of time will be accessible in the planogramming software.

To begin, start with a "heat map" of the planogram to show where sales are generating on the planogram. Begin with unit sales or volume. The products with the highest sales will be green while those with the lowest sales will be red. This quickly starts to indicate where the most productive products are positioned on the shelf. You can do the same for dollar sales or profit. Look for common locations that show where slow movers are collecting on the planogram. Sharing these graphic images with your merchants while they are planning their future assortment can sometimes validate their intentions about discontinuing slow sellers.

Provide space productivity reports to your merchants. While they will have access to sales reports and inventory turns measurements, they are unlikely to have any visibility into the amount of space products are using to deliver those results. For example, a merchant may not see that two items with the same performance may produce that performance in very different merchandising schemes, depending on the stores carrying the item:

- *Item A $200 average weekly sales Item B $200 average weekly sales*
- *Item A In planograms for 50 stores Item B In planograms for 100 stores*

Therefore,
Item A $400 average weekly sales/store selling
Item B $200 average weekly sales/store selling

Or they may not understand the differences in the facings and merchandising on the planograms:

- *Item A $200 average weekly sales Item B $200 average weekly sales*
- *Item A an average of 10" in planograms Item B an average of 20" in planograms*

Therefore,

  Item A producing $20/linear inch

  Item B producing $10/linear inch

Put both the stores selling AND the space productivity and Item A and Item B are producing very differently:

- *Item A $200 average weekly sales Item B $200 average weekly sales*
- *Item A an average of 10" in 50 stores Item B an average of 20" in 100 stores*

Therefore,

  Item A producing $40/linear inch per store selling

  Item B producing $10/linear inch per store selling

How does that happen? How could 2 items with similar sales in aggregate, have such different space productivity metrics? There could be many root causes:

- Despite having enough space planned, Item B may have been out of stock in some of the 100 stores that were to carry the item. Perhaps some of that customer demand transferred to Item A.
- Item B may have a higher propensity to be sold online that Item A. If the merchant is looking at sales across all channels, Item B could have a significant part of its customer demand fulfilled online and not in stores – leading to higher total sales but lower store space productivity.
- Item A could more frequent delivery and replenishment cycles in the stores than Item B. So despite having a smaller shelf footprint, if it is an item that is replenished every day, it can turn faster and boost its space productivity over Item B which may only be fulfilled semi-monthly and requires more shelf space to account for demand between delivery cycles. Many times, DSD items will have a higher space productivity rate than

normally replenished items for this very reason.

- Space may have been misallocated in past planograms where Item B was given more space than necessary and placed in more planogram versions than Item A. Use your analysis and collaboration with your category managers to suggest that store space productivity would improve with a better balance for Item A and B in both space utilization and planogram version allocation.

The most common micro space productivity metric is sales/linear foot. Linear foot (or linear inch) measures the width of the product as it faces the customer – on a shelf, on a peg hook or in a bin – and divides its sales performance for that space. Linear space can be aggregated across stores for a full chain metric.

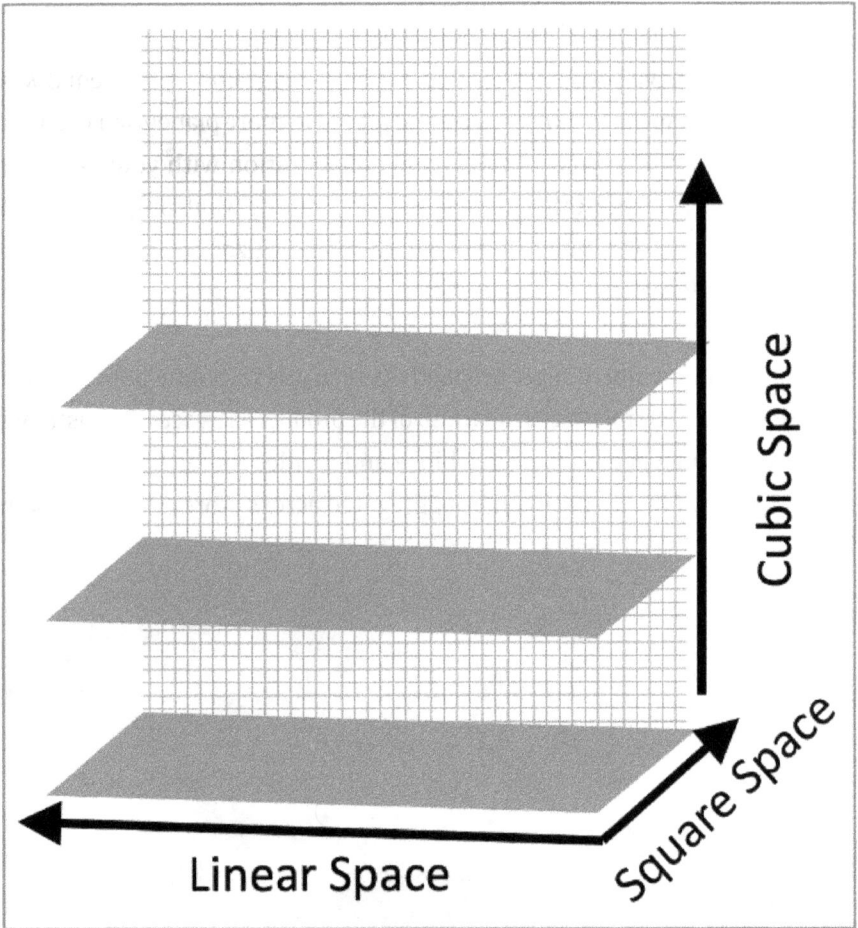

Figure 20: The Dimensions used for measuring micro space

As you conduct space analyses, be prepared for a challenge on the metric you use. Because there are three possible denominators in a space metric (linear, square or cubic space) there will nearly always be someone who will want to use a different way of measuring space.

Measurement	Pro's	Con's
Linear Space	Accurately represents the visual presentation to shoppers. Can be aggregated across planograms and stores.	Can penalize large items with low price points over small items with high price points
Square Space	Accurately represents the shelf space required to merchandise an item.	Can penalize products that are merchandised on deep shelves or long peg hooks. Can underrepresent air space in planograms.
Cubic Space	Fully represents the total space required to merchandise an item	Can penalize products on tall gondolas or perimeter walls. Can penalize large items with low price points over small items with high price points

As you can see there are pros and cons to all methods. The important thing is that your organization select one metric and apply it consistently. Varying the metric by business line or location can create more discord. Try to focus your business partners on the importance of having a consistent approach over time and that the real benefit is in the trajectory of the measurement (improving space productivity over time.)

To make progress in analyzing a single planogram, ensure that your sales data and integrations are correct for the time period and stores that are assigned to the planogram. Review the high and low space performers in the set. Usually, planogrammers use highlights within their software tool for a visual cue about top and bottom sellers, top profit contributors, and space productivity to make facing adjustments and recommendations to category managers about items to be removed. Your organization should have a template of standard reports, graphs and highlights that provide the most common insights into the planogram performance. Understand when to use the various tools at your disposal. Some of the most common reports to include in a space packet for a category manager are Space performance by brand or manufacturer. Both of which are key to fair share analyses.

The "Fair Share" Concept in Planograms

One of the most common analyses is the comparison of space allocation to performance to measure the balance across the two. The basic idea being that if a product represents 30 percent of the sales, it ought to have 30 percent of the space. This "fair share" is regularly promoted by suppliers. To be fair, suppliers are often measured and rewarded on their ability to secure their brand's "fair share" of space in their accounts. But "fair share" can be a flawed if it is the only framework for a space analysis.

It makes sense to begin with a "fair share" space allocation. It can be useful for the big picture. For example, if you had to complete a snack food planogram, it would be helpful to know that potato chips are 55% of the sales, tortilla chips are 25% of the sales and popcorn is 20% of the sales. Making sure that you had those ratios as you begin to allocate space is important. But what would you do if you knew that popcorn sales in the marketplace is down -15% while tortilla chips are up a whopping +22%. What would "fair share" look like then?

So "fair share" should only be relied on as a foundation. But then many different considerations should be layered on top of the "fair share" of space allocation. Considerations such as:

- Sales trends in the market including flavor, color and style trends. Planograms are built for the future. So, it is important for planograms to lead trends in aggressively reducing declining items and leaning into emerging trends.
- Changing demographics and long-term changes for a retailer's customers. Neighborhoods can change quickly, and a changing shopper base can dramatically change demand for products.

- Supplier commitments for exclusive items, new product allocations and customer promotions that could change sales patterns. Vendors and category managers can enter into agreements that determine the space allocations that certain products will have on the shelf.
- Strategic business plans. A strategic change – say to increase super-premium offerings and exit low-priced goods – means that space allocations need to exceed the limits of "fair share."
- Private brand placement and allocation. Despite perhaps having lower sales, a retailer's private brand may have a mandated placement or space allocation that purposefully exceeds its "fair share."
- Delivery cycles. If products on a planogram have different delivery cycles, then reviewing a planogram for each brand's "fair share" will over allocate space to the products with the most frequent replenishment cycles. Instead of fair share of sales, it would be better to allocate space based on a required inventory service level so that the space is optimized.
- Packout Requirements. A retail operator can have a requirement to hold a minimum of a case and a half on the shelf, despite low sales levels. In those situations, products will get more than their fair share of shelf space, due to the operational mandates.
- Limiting out of stocks. If there are suppliers that are unreliable due to supply chain disruptions or have a pattern of non-performance, their "fair share" of space may be reduced to limit stockout liability for the retailer. Until the supplier can demonstrate predictable on-time deliveries, providing their products with shelf space may be the same as planning for shelf outages.
- Shrink and theft. If there are items that have higher appeal for theft and shoplifting, they may purposefully receive less than their "fair share" of shelf space. To limit the cost of shrink, retailers can choose to minimize the item's presentation at the shelf.

Days of Supply and Pack Out

As a planogrammer reviews space allocation, reviewing the number of days of supply on the shelf or DOS refers to how many days it will take for the stock on the shelf to run out if sales continue at the same rate as recent sales. Knowing the days of supply helps determine how much shelf space to allocate to products. You don't want to be constantly restocking fast-moving products, nor do you want to dedicate too much space to less popular products. So DOS is a good regulator. Your goal is to get your days of supply to be equal to or just barely greater than your frequency of delivery and restocking.

When you are in perfect balance, the inventory turns at a predictable rate. Dated inventory has less chance of hitting expiration dates on the shelf. Fast movers are replenished before shoppers clear out the shelf.

Ideally, if you re-stocked your products every 5 days, each item on the planogram would have about 6 days of supply on the shelf (so that they never went completely empty before you restock it.) You need a little buffer. Like the note above about Delivery cycles, the point is that the DOS for each item should roughly correspond and cover the expected shopper demand between replenishment cycles for that item in the store. At the very least, your goals should be to reduce the spread of DOS for the items on the shelf.

A way to evaluate whether you are making progress in this area is to compare the DOS range before and after remerchandising a planogram. If you reduce the range (reduce facings on the slowest sellers and increase facings on the fast movers) you can reach a better equilibrium in inventory planning.

It isn't just facings that can change a product's stock levels on the shelf. Whether or not you stack items (like cans of cat food) or cap items (laying a box on end across the top of front-facings boxes) changes the shelf capacity. Just remember that the goal is to transform how the product gets merchandised in the physical stores. It does not matter if you attain your goals at the computer when building planograms if the merchandising direction will not be followed in the stores. Stay real.

Besides balancing space presentation for shopper demand and improving inventory turn, planograms also need to meet operational objectives to make the stores easier to operate. Store team members have relentless pressure to provide excellent customer service and build relationships with shoppers. That's difficult if they have to spend all their time stocking shelves.

Many retailer operators will set a pack out requirement for products on the shelves to ensure that there will be a home location for an entire shipment of an item received at the store. If a product comes in a case of 24, but the planogram only has room for 16 items on the shelf, store team members will have to "upstock" the remaining 8 items, shove them into the set by adding more facings or return them to the backroom. All of which leads to confusion and "lost inventory" in the store. To make it easier for shelf stockers, a puckout minimum will require planogrammers to increase facings on slow sellers to meet the inventory capacity threshold.

As a planogrammer who is managing one single planogram, analysis is important to review space productivity with category managers. That analysis can indicate items that should be removed or change their space allocation or store assignments during the assortment planning process. Fair share analysis combined with a number of forward-looking forecasts are used to allocate space within the planogram to anticipated shopper demand. Days of supply analyses can increase or reduce the inventory turn rates by examining the shelf inventory capacity. Finally, a pack out review will ensure that the planogram will be easier to maintain in the stores. Every planogram should have these basic reviews and analysis during the production stage before release for further action.

Planogram Analysis - The Planogram Project

We just reviewed the key steps for every individual planogram. But most micro space planners work in groups of planograms at once. They work a planogram project that includes all of the planogram versions aligned to a single category. In that sense, there is a level of continuity and alignment across the entire project that planogrammers must be vigilant to deliver before they accomplish the transition.

Analyses for a complete project focus on two main areas: operational consistencies and financial impacts.

Amongst the most common analyses for a planogrammer to conduct before completing a project is an overarching summary of the items added and deleted by planogram version. Experienced planogrammers are vigilant to ensure that there is logical consistency in the merchandising variations. Deleted items must be removed from every planogram. New items added must be consistent and reported to inventory allocation who will order the first case shipment in advance of the execution date. Critical promotional items must be available in every planogram so that a chain-wide sale can be supported in every store location.

Modern space planning systems can assist with that detailed work by automating most of those changes. Using scripts or workflows, a planogrammer can use instruction blocks to ensure that all the items are properly accounted for. Which frees up more time for the planogrammer to do more valuable analysis to find pockets of opportunity in their store merchandising.

Operational reports can highlight possible execution issues. A pre- and post- fixture report highlights any new fixtures that stores must secure before they can execute the plan. Shelf adjustments, new dividers or other fixture elements that take time to implement should be accounted for in estimating the time it will take to complete the planogram change. Sharing the scope of change including those fixture changes as well as placement changes and number of items removed, added and relocated is critical for the team that will help stores create a schedule for the change. Finally, reporting for the shelf inventory capacity by item is key to the inventory team who are charged with maintaining a well-stocked store.

Since our work is data-driven and stored within files, all of this data can be made available in real-time to other functions that need to reference it. Whether your space planning system is in a database that is located on premises, an externally hosted system with cloud access or in flat files on a network drive, the data should be exposed so that other systems and authorized users can access the data at will for their work. If your installation requires you to create reports, it is important that the reporting is as automated as possible to boost your productivity and reporting accuracy.

The importance of the financial reporting from space planning can be overlooked in the focus of operational data handoffs. One key data element that space planning systems know and can share with merchandise financial planners, CM's and the CFO is the inventory value changes caused by a planogram project. Because a planogramming system knows the exact inventory quantities planned for each item by store and the cost of each item, space planners can run a pre-/post- inventory projection to estimate the change in the cost of goods to make a planogram change.

For example, let's imagine that we are working on the Toys category. Our Category Manager decides to stop carrying jigsaw puzzles in favor of a new line of electronic toys. In our example, let's make it easy and say that the jigsaw puzzles were in a six-foot section and that the entire section is being converted to the new electronic toys. Jigsaw puzzles are physically large and have a relatively low price point. Which means, in the past, we could fill that entire six-foot section with jigsaw puzzles for about $900 per store. (That is measured in COGS - cost of goods sold. The sales of those items would have been about $1400 in retail sales.) Our new electronics toy line is both more expensive than jigsaw puzzles and each item is smaller than a jigsaw puzzle. Which means we will need more units of the new electronic line to fill the six feet. We can use our planogramming system to evaluate the COGS of each item and the expected inventory required to fill the set and report that it will now cost $3600 to fill the same six feet of space in our stores. (Yielding $5750 in retail sales.) Clearly, that space will become much more productive if we can extract $5750 in sales where we once only produced $1400 in sales. But we have a 400% increase in the money we will need to pay for that inventory before we will start to see those sales. Our finance team needs to be aware that they need to find the funds for this investment. If we have 400 stores, it is the difference between a chain-wide $360,000 inventory investment and a $1.44 million investment!

Another critical project level review helps the inventory and replenishment team align and inform distribution center resources about changes to item placement by store. DCs operate efficiently by maximizing inventory throughput. The goal is to turn inventory as quickly as possible and move product into and out of the DC with little delay. Afterall, unless they are fulfilling online orders, customers do not buy products from a DC. As a result, Distribution Centers are set up with a focus on reducing the amount of time products are in the facility. In fully mature operations, even slot placement matters so that forklifts are traveling the least distance possible to fill orders. Naturally, products that will be replenished by a DC to all stores will be in more store shipments than items that are only going to be carried in a small number of stores. DC managers will assign slots accordingly. Accordingly, project level reporting by DC is a critical downstream data feed that space planning systems create.

As a space planner reviews a project across the chain, one of the most common reviews is identifying and addressing outlier stores. For every project, there will be outlier stores that are so unusual in either their configuration or performance that they must be handled as individual instances and not just a variation of a planogram version. An easy way to identify outlier stores is to review the sales per linear or square foot for the category or the average item's space productivity for the category and compare each store to the chain average.

Some stores are nearly always outliers no matter which category project is involved. Stores that are flagship stores with unique fixtures and sign packages are usually outliers. So are stores that are test locations for new prototypes. Some stores are so unusual in their geography or shopper demographic that they are always outliers. Examples include stores that are directly adjacent to major transportation hubs where shopping is heaviest during commuting hours and there is little parking so that large items are almost never purchased. Or stores that are part of a large tourist destination location like Disney Springs, Times Square or The Shoppes at Caesars in Las Vegas. Retailers create a list of "usual suspects" and almost always create separate assortment plans and merchandising plans for those unique outlier stores. Since they behave so differently from the balance of the chain, it is not unusual to have them segregated when conducting analyses as well. Thus, sales per square foot analyses for the chain may exempt airport location stores or other outlier stores.

But for each category, there can also be unusual outlier stores that ought to be researched and evaluated for each project. For example, some categories can have unusual swings because of their location near colleges, dog parks, hospitals or resorts. Those stores will perform in a standard fashion as a whole, but may show wildly unusual patterns in beer sales, dog treats, floral bouquets or sunscreen. While those outliers overindex in sales performance, other stores can be outliers because of their unusual underperformance in sales. For example, when a grocery store is adjacent to a pet super store in a shopping center, it is common for its pet food sales in the grocery store to be far below normal. Therefore, competition can cause outliers.

But it is for the space planner who is charged with driving merchandising that will satisfy shoppers to review outlier stores to look for any situations where the merchandising itself is contributing to a store's unusual performance. In reviewing a project, a space planner should first pull all outlier stores and review their floorplans and fixturing for any disruptive pattern. For example:

1. Does the category placement have an unusual location in the store compared to the balance of the chain? Look for categories that are placed apart from their natural adjacencies which may be causing confusion for shoppers. Like when Diapers are placed with household paper products instead of Baby Care.

2. Does the planogram have an unusual configuration within the store? Examples include when a category "wraps" from one aisle around a back endcap and into the next aisle. Shoppers can be confused and only see a part of the assortment selection when they are standing "in front" of the planogram. Or when a planogram must span an inner or outer corner for the same reason.

3. Does the planogram have unusual fixturing that may make the category hard to shop? Bins, pusher systems or drawers can all become difficult to shop when shoppers cannot see all the merchandise or have a hard time accessing products. Shelves that are unusually tall or deep can "hide" products on the shelf making "visual out of stocks."

4. Are there singular elements in the store that make the category difficult to access or shop? Columns, sign holders, electronic displays and bulk stack locations can disrupt shoppers more than help them and can interrupt the expect shopping pattern.

5. Are there remainders of past tests that need to be "cleaned up?" It is a sad reality that many times stores are selected to be in a market test – for fixtures, signs, layouts or other components – and are left to languish long after the test ended. Without an effort to return the store back to the standard, the store operates and performs differently than others in the fleet.

If a space planner finds these unusual merchandising issues, the next step is to raise the issues and see if there are ways to improve any contributing factors. If merchandise can shift or if there can be better adjacencies is key. Often store team members or district managers themselves have seen and recognize the issues and may have recommendations. Reach out to operations to see if something can be adjusted quickly. Otherwise, go to the floor planning team or the remodeling team and see if changes can be noted and prioritized for the next time the store will be included in a major merchandising effort.

For space planners, reviewing the outlier stores as they prepare a project is key to creating merchandising plans that store operators can adopt. When retailers ignore the unique properties of outlier stores, they can suboptimize positive shopping habits in the best performing stores. Providing those stores with a "normal" planogram could create out of stocks for best sellers. Conversely, Not addressing merchandising issues for bottom-performing outliers can exacerbate sales declines. Once a space planner identifies the outliers, partnering with category managers, operations and floor planning may help address the issue.

In the case where the store behaves as an outlier, but there are no contributing elements from a space planning point of view, raise the store's performance with the replenishment team and the category manager. It may be that the store is serviced by a unique distributor or that the replenishment cycle is incorrect. Perhaps there are other issues that teams could address if they realized the unusual nature of the store's performance. During the category review and space planning cycle is the best time to address outlier issues.

As the space planner nears completion of a project an easy way to review the project's effectiveness is to conduct these comparisons to understand how the project adds value for the retailer and its shoppers.

First review the entire chain and then perhaps each region or district to show:

1. The total count of unique items on the planogram, the number of items added, and the number of items removed. (assortment churn) That measure the overall number of items assorted on the planograms and the level of item churn. That churn metric is important to help the company understand the possible need for more (or less) frequent planogram changes. If churn ratios for a category are regularly much higher than the rest of the categories, it may be an indication that it is more dynamic than other categories and needs more frequent POG updates. The churn ratio is also helpful in understanding the impact the planogram change may have on stores and shoppers.

2. The assortment rank range of each planogram version. Let's imagine that a CM provided an assortment that ranged from item #1-#250. Ideally, the smallest planogram would contain items #1-#25 and the largest would have items #1-#250. There would be a problem if a mid-sized POG had only items #12-150. This measures whether planograms are focused on top-selling items or if small and mid-sized planograms are carrying too broad a range for their size.

3. A mean item rank for each planogram per- and post-execution. In other words, if a planogram had a mean rank of 68 before the planogram change, but a mean rank of 54 after the planogram change, it would mean that the company was properly pruning lower ranked items to carry a higher concentration of better selling ones. This helps forecast whether the new planogram will support greater customer demand than the previous version did. It can guide a Category Manager and the space planning team to focus on planograms that may be moving in the wrong direction and adjust.

4. The total count of items that are identified as "top items" and top item churn. Plus, the highest ranking of a removed item. Like the assortment churn in #1 above, this measures the churn of products that the retailer has identified as a top item. This could be the top 50 or 100 items, for example. It helps flag to Category Managers to situations where they ought to account for change sin top sellers by replacing them with equal or better items. Sometimes these top seller changes are

intentional (like when an 8 ounce and a 12-ounce item are both in the top 50 but a CM wishes to increase revenue and eliminates the 8-ounce item in hopes that shoppers will trade up to the 12-ounce item.) But if a planogram version somehow eliminates a top seller without intent, this quick review will point it out.

5. Where the retailer has a focus on private label products, a total count for the private label items and the percentage of items and space devoted to the private label product by planogram version. This makes sure that private labels are represented on the various planograms in a way that the Category Manager intended. If private brands are over- or under-represented in a particular planogram version, then the category manager or space planner can adjust.

6. The mean (average) pack out by planogram version before and after the planogram change. This measures whether the overall planogram is becoming easier or more difficult to replenish for our store team members.

7. The mean (average) days of supply before and after the planogram change. Also, the highest and lowest days of supply for any item on a planogram version after the planogram change. This measure if the inventory levels on the new planogram meet the goal and if any adjustments are needed in space or assortment changes to ensure that the inventory turn will be at an acceptable level after the planogram change.

These seven reports/analyses can be part of a pre-approval package that each category's planogram change team monitors before approving planograms for publishing to the stores and other downstream systems. If a retailer has refined their merchandising to reflect clusters instead of regions as a way to version planograms, then each cluster can have their planograms reviewed in this fashion. Ideally, these post-merchandising reports and graphs are automated and can be accessed easily within the space planning reporting interface for users or anyone else with permission to view the reports.

Space Productivity – Macro Space Optimization

If you learn one thing from this book, know this:

> *If you want to improve the market share for your brands and shift profits within a category, make planogram improvements. If you want to change the trajectory of your stock price and make profit shifts for your entire chain, make floor plan improvements.*

Measuring, optimizing and executing floor plan changes are the most complicated and costly resource change a retailer can make. Think how easy it is to change the prices in a POS system, add or remove media channels to an advertising plan and add or remove store associate hours from a month's labor budget. While they would take some time, they can happen quickly, and early responses can be adjusted up or down to hit the "right" level. Contrast that with the cost of fixtures, shopper disruption, inventory shifts and assortment changes that occur when a chain changes the location, adjacencies or space allocation for a category across their stores. It can take a year or more to analyze, plan and execute a store change. And if the change does not produce the right outcomes, the risk is very high.

Simply planning macro space optimization is a deeply integrated activity for retailers as this graphic illustrates:

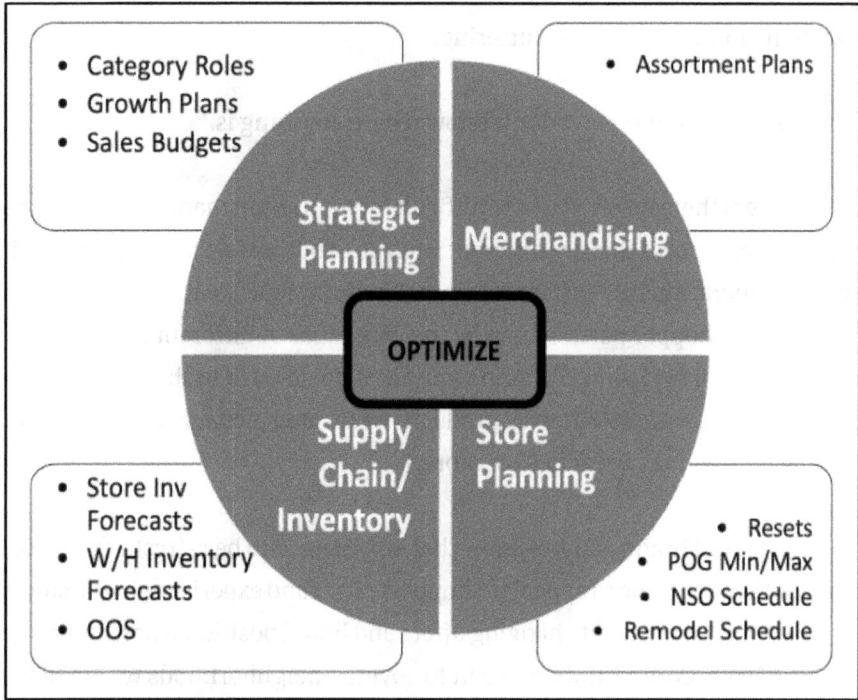

Figure 21: A model for integrated macro space optimization

Maybe it is for that reason, executives shy away from the effort to maximize store layouts to produce better results. You see it all the time when retailers begin to open new concept stores that "right size" their departments and layouts yet hold back from retrofitting stores that are already in the market with those optimized layouts. I cannot help but wonder if another contributing factor is the high degree of executive churn that disincentivizes a merchandising executive from championing such an expensive endeavor. But given enough time, executive churn and new store openings/acquisitions, it is not unusual for retailers to have a menagerie of stores on the market that have wildly different footprint and space allocations.

For shoppers, it can be disorienting to visit a brand they know well in their home market while travelling to learn that a store in a different market has a completely different look and feel. As they try to navigate the new store location, you'll hear them muttering,

"This isn't like my store. I don't know where anything is."

For retailers themselves, it can be difficult for multi-unit managers to operate and optimize stores that are different from one another in presentation. Their internal operations are different to run. Checkout lane positions, stockroom access, and shopper patterns can be the root cause of different shrink levels, replenishment cycles and sales in stores that are located in the same market. And they can have very different productivity through no fault of the excellent managers that may work in each store.

Marketers and brand experts know that stores need to be refreshed and stay up to date to continue to appeal to shoppers. The rand experience in the stores need to evolve to support changing offers and brand positions that marketing plans deliver. Competitors move in to coveted neighborhoods where fickle shoppers can abandon long-standing loyal shopping patterns. Categories are dynamic and change over time as new innovations and marketing plans uncover and meet emerging shopper needs. All of which means that stores need to reflect that same dynamism to remain interesting to shoppers.

So how can space planning help to make this important, high risk/high reward effort more accessible? First, there must be a commitment to measure space productivity and identify opportunities and value pools that could be accessed through a floor plan change. Second, the space system and practice have to be built from the ground up to make measurements accurate and reliable. Third, there must be a scorecard that indicates the action and decisions that must be made to improve store space productivity. Finally, there must be a financial executive process where space allocation decisions can be presented to the company decision-makers who can evaluate the opportunities against other capital expenditures and prioritize the investments. All of which means that a retailer must be operating at a Level 5 on a maturity scale for Macro Space, Analytics and Executive Business

Planning.

First, the company and its merchandising leaders must agree that there is value in measuring space productivity and that they want to assess the opportunities that could be addressed if they were to make store space changes. If the company leaders cannot or will not invest in the costs to remodel a significant portion of the store fleet, then the work to measure each store and their business is unnecessary. Presuming that retail leaders are ready for this effort, there are two ways to address store changes at a macro level:

1. Evaluate the performance of categories, departments and planograms across all stores to identify holistic changes that should ripple across the entire fleet to improve performance. Think of an analysis that compares the tradeoff for the entire chain if the space for bovine-based dairy product were reduced in favor of expanding plant-based dairy products.
2. Evaluate each store against all the other stores in the chain to identify the particular stores that have the most improvements to be gained through a remodel that re-allocates space within that store. This can be particularly helpful when stores have been in the market for many decades or when there is a constrained budget for tackling remodel efforts.

To deliver reliable data for either effort, the space planning team must have a stable system, clean data and a consistent methodology that supports macro space analysis.

First, there must be accurate floor plans. Stores change regularly. There are planogram changes as well as the items that inhabit promotional and seasonal locations. There may be outdoor merchandise placements for live plants, seasonal furnishings, outdoor equipment or other goods that are purchased from areas that are outside the store sales floor. So accurate "floor plans" can actually include areas outside of the sales floor. Again, the use of robots, mounted cameras and image recognition and modern space planning systems that can ingest photo files are key to keeping floor plans up to date.

Second, there is the concept of space allocation over time which must be accounted for in space data. Most retailers do a poor job of accounting for changes to space allocations over time. Planograms have lifecycles with start and end dates so that a product that had 2 facings in the first half of the year but then expanded to 5 facings in the second half of the year are captured in the planogram data over time. But floor plans are not always stored that way. If so, they are not regularly updated with the promotional space allocations that can be such a disruptive element in macro space analysis.

Promotional space is an outlier factor in many macro space analytics, yet if can be accounted for with proper planning.

Understand that promotional space can be a primary sales driver for some categories. Let's contrast two businesses in a grocery chain. The first is Spices and Seasonings. The second is Bottled Water sold by the case. Let's say that both experience a 12X lift when placed on promotion. Spices and Seasonings have a low average volume and a small cube. Meaning that they have a small amount of space compared to their weight and that storing them and replenishing them takes up little space or effort. Contrast that with bulky, heavy water cases with their high cube and substantial effort to store and replenish. Spices can fairly easily support their 12X sales lift from their home location. The macro space allocation for spices even through high promotional sales weeks are stable enough that all sales can be attributed to their planogrammed space allocation. Water, meanwhile, cannot support a 12X lift from its home location. Instead, pallets of water may be stacked in the store vestibule, along perimeter walls, endcaps or in wide walkways throughout the store. Which means that assigning the sales for water to only the planogrammed space locations would grossly undercount the amount of space that water needs to support its sales. To accurately measure water's space productivity, analysis must include the additional promotional locations that supported its promotional sales.

Also, each store will not have the same promotional locations. End cap counts will differ, entryways and walkways are different. Aisle widths vary. Then the best course is to create a standard vocabulary across all stores for naming promotional locations and then tying promotions to those locations. For example, every store has a vestibule. But not every store can merchandise the same quantity of products there. Every store has front-facing, high-traffic end caps. Every store has back-facing, low-volume end caps. Stores may designate placements along walkways for pallets or floor stands. Each of those can be labelled or numbered. Each store then, can have specific promotional locations that are known on the floor plan like this:

If we imagine that stores set promotional locations every 2 weeks, then each location in each store could have a product or products assigned to it 104 times throughout the year. Some products may remain on a location for many weeks. And some products may change but the category always stays the same (like a Cereal endcap.) But the point is, when macro space locations and promotional plans are integrated, each location in a store can be assigned to a product or at least a category for macro space productivity measurements. If it is managed in a database that is created through a relationship between stores and their eligible locations and promotional assignments, the floor plans do not need to be updated every 2 weeks. Only the promotional assignments need to be updated.

This same methodology and data structure can be leverage to account for seasonal outdoor spaces that stores use throughout the year. A side yard or sidewalk that is used to merchandise grills, lawnmowers, mulch, live plants, fences, or other goods can be measured and assigned to each store. Products are then allocated to those locations and the store's overall "selling space" will fluctuate over time.

Too many retailers have not built a dataset that accounts for variation in space allocation over time. Space data must always account for a time dimension in the data. Be warned against data structures that are restricted to a point in time because it will cause distortion and errors in macro space optimization.

Another issue in macro space is simply what to measure. Besides accounting for home locations, promotional locations, and seasonal space changes. There are shared space areas that either need to be allocated or removed from analysis. Think of things like the space in an aisleway, the customer service counter, check lane areas and their queuing space for shoppers in line, the back room and all of the other square footage of a store's footprint.

Most retailers immediately remove the backroom from all space productivity analyses. But if there is an intention of evaluating all stores against one another through a lens of rent and leasing fees, then the backroom may be relevant in macro space analytics. It will not change the productivity comparison across categories within a store. But it can change the productivity comparison across stores.

Aisleways are more problematic. One practice is to cut all aisleways down the middle and apply the empty aisle and walkway space to the businesses directly adjacent to the space. Afterall, shoppers need a place to stand in front of the bedding department to select their sheets. The space that the shoppers stand in should be accounted for. And that bedding would not sell if shoppers could not stand before them making a selection. But this method is especially troublesome for categories that are routinely placed along the widest throughways while other categories are habitually placed deep inside departments where there are narrower aisles. If your stores have a wide range of walkways and departments, consider a few things:

1. Is the space that a department or category requires based on shopper

needs or architecture? Shoppers need more space to walk around furnishings and to sit in armchairs and sofas. Which is why wide spaces ought to be assigned to the seating department. But for a shopper to select table lamps, they may only need to have the standard width aisle. Anytime that table lamps are on a larger-than-normal aisleway, perhaps the size should be reduced to standard and the remainder placed in the yet-to-be-defined proportional "shared space" allocation.

2. Are some businesses destination categories and such high image categories that they deserve being in the wide throughway locations? Consider a home décor category that changes 6 times per year in a big box retailer. The category helps define the seasonal assortment for the entire store and is a destination for most shoppers. So, while it may be "penalized" with such a wide walkway adjacency, it also benefits by being in such a high traffic area that drives high visibility and high sales. So perhaps it deserves to have the entire aisleway allocated to its total space measurements.

Each retailer will need to look at its prototypical department placements and the strategy behind their location. Then create a set of guiding principles for allocating aisleway and walkway space that respects the strategy for placing businesses where they are in the store.

Shared spaces are literally spaces that the store needs to operate but are not necessarily supporting any specific business line. One of the best examples is the space taken by cashiers, a return desk and customer service. Certainly, a retailer could include all aisleways, the vestibule and all other areas that do not have merchandising. Generally, retailers who include these spaces in their analysis proportionately allocate the space back to all business lines within the store based on dollar sales or unit volume. Units may be a more fair method when some products in the store retail for $2.99 while other retail for $2999.00. Be thoughtful about some shared space allocations, however. For example, if there is space for diners to eat what they have purchased on a hot bar or salad bar, that space should probably be proportionately allocated back to the quick serve food items diners are consuming in those spaces and not to baby diapers, for example. If there is a repairs desk, allocate its space back to the businesses that have repairs done in a proportionate method. If your stores have a professional sales counter, a custom ordering counter, a warranty desk or any other spaces that are meant to service a limited number of businesses from the store, their space should be only allocated back to those limited businesses.

So far, we have been talking about making sure that the denominator of all space productivity measurements is accurate (the amount of space.) But we also need to attend to the numerator (the sales or profits being divided across businesses.) Again, look at every single revenue line for a store. If there are extended warranties, repairs, service and installation fees, tailoring fees, or any other money that a store can receive, those revenue lines must be proportionately reallocated back to the proper businesses when measuring space productivity. Let's say, for example, that a home building center had a $1.2 million revenue line called "custom orders." And that the custom order desk and kiosks took up 4,000 sf in a store. It would be important to know that 20% of those custom orders were for siding, 25% were for lumber and 55% were for flooring/carpet. The $1.2 million in revenue and the 4,000 sf should be apportioned then to siding, lumber and flooring to accurately account for the productivity of those businesses.

A basic mistake is to account for everything listed above, but then compare a simple ratio of sales or profit over space. In other words, to compare the sales per square foot or the profit per cubic foot across the businesses in a store and surrender space from the lowest performers awarding that space to the highest performers. As some level, this is likely to improve the store's overall productivity if there are divergent extremes in category performances. But the smarter way to look at awarding space is to consider marginal return on the space. This evaluates the performance decay curves of every business and seeks to harmonize and optimize each business line.

Here is a real example. In a consumer electronics department, cell phone charging cables had the highest gross revenue per square foot of the entire department. They took up 8' of linear space returned $1255 per foot per month. Amongst the lowest performing businesses were landline phones. They took up 20' of space and returned $418 per foot per month. If you were to make a surrender/award decision on those two data points, you might take space from landline phones and give it to call phone cables. However, the decay curve on the cables was very steep. There are only a few kinds of charging cables, and they take up very little space. So, while the first foot of space for cables returned an astounding $3277 per foot per month, the 8th foot only contributed $145 per foot per month. Overall, it returned $1255 for the entire 8 feet, but almost all of that productivity came in the first four feet.

Meanwhile, landline phones are quirky. People who want them really love the novelty of having a phone. They see them as a fashion statement as a much as a working communication device. So, they come in a wide range of colors and licenses like M&M's®, superheroes, Muppets™ and more. There are vintage phones, clear phones, round phones, corded and cordless phones. And shoppers love to select the perfect phone for their room and style. So, the decay curve on landline phones is very long and flat. Each additional foot of space seems to only add more selection for shoppers who find the perfect phone in the store. So, while the first foot of land line phones contributed $812 per foot per month, the 20th foot of space contributed $280 per foot per month.

Which means when we compare the marginal return between these two businesses to decide which would make better use of one more additional foot of space, we can see that the next foot of cell phone charging cables would only yield $145 per foot or less. While the landline phones would use that foot of space to yield $280 per foot or less. Hence, the better choice would be to give any additional space to landline phones – not cell phone cables.

Evaluating degrading productivity decay curves can be difficult when prod-ucts are not merchandised in neat increments where the first foot is the most productive, the second foot is the next set, etc. For data analysts to develop clarity, they can begin with item level space productivity (comparing item level sales per square foot or linear foot) and then decile that data to create a kind of space decay proxy. If it also accounts for promotional space over time, seasonal space, prorated shared space and additional revenue streams originating from the business, then it is superior to a standard sales per square foot measurement.

When launching a macro space optimization effort, the most overlooked obstacle is staging the data. The data scrubbing, attributing, extraction, transformation and preparation is a difficult task when there are portions of the store like apparel or produce that will have different data than the planogrammed areas in center store or hardlines. Do not underestimate the effort in collecting, cleansing and normalizing the data prior to analyzing it. Too often, analytics teams rush to select the most sophisticated analysis they can support and spend resources selecting the best methodology to conduct the macro space optimization only to discover that the data set is rubbish. This is an area where thoughtful consideration up front will pay off in huge dividends once the organization starts to analyze the data.

The BIG picture: Analyzing the Fleet

Extending our analysis lens even further out, there is a regularly conducted macro analysis for retail executives to analyze each store's performance in the entire chain. The goal is to identify the stores that are most likely to show a marked improvement with investment into their physical location. On the table can be everything from a quick remerchandising and layout change without changing the traffic flow to a complete remodel with an entirely new look and feel. Also on the table can be difficult decisions like relocating a store or closing it entirely. And while these decisions are made above the level of a journeyman space planner, the executive team relies on space productivity analyses and other space measurements to make the costly decisions about how to manage an entire store fleet.

It begins with regular reporting for every store compared to its cohorts across the chain to identify leading and lagging stores. Store contribution reports are at the most macro level and are useful when identifying stores that have exceedingly high or low labor expenses, rent expenses, utility expenses, shrink expenses, and other overall operational fees. But embedded within that evaluation should be space productivity measurements for the front of the house. Whether using sales per square foot or Gross Margin Return on Space (GMROS), the KPI needs to be fairly applied to every store so that a valid comparison can be made.

First things first: expect large stores to have lower productivity rates compared to small stores. If large stores have expanded space without expanded selections and experiences that will cause shoppers to buy more than the same selection/experience in "normal sized" stores, the effect is to merely spread the same sales across more space. Naturally, space productivity will decline in the biggest stores.

To address this issue, consider the problem from a few perspectives:

1. Is the shopping experience more enjoyable and is the store easier to operate when there is more space? If the experience of shopping in the largest stores is creating more loyal, satisfied shoppers, then any change may be unnecessary. As long as sales remain at an expected rate, there may be little to do to improve space productivity without adding in additional selections or businesses.

2. Does it make sense to expand assortments or lines of business for the largest stores to make their retail sales floors as efficient as smaller stores? If there is reason to believe that there is additional profit – *and that the cost of adding products for only a few stores will be maintain margins*

– consider adding an extended range into those stores or additional business lines.

One way to add businesses to your largest stores without deteriorating your inventory investments and turn is to partner with others to create either store-within-a-store models. When the selected partner is accountable for inventory and marketing, it can add an interesting new solution for your shoppers and provide insights into their behavior that you may not have learned otherwise. In fact, store-within-a-store practices are one of the best ways that retailers can evaluate possible new business lines before extending their own resources to see what a real-world shopper test can deliver.

Another way is to add a consignment model to the extended range that you add to the store. Offer suppliers the opportunity to sell a new line or more variations of their current line in your largest stores when they agree to a consignment model. In a consignment model, the inventory belongs to the supplier until it is sold at the register. It is the act of selling the product that transfers the ownership to the retailer who then "pays for the stock" as it is sold to the final customer. This is a way to bring more choices into your largest stores without needing to take on the risk of the excess inventory.

1. Are there new experiences to bring into your largest stores that will not improve sales *per se*, but could improve loyalty and dwell time in the store? Community rooms, coffee shops, in-store dining tables and improved high-end experiences are all ways to make the store a destination. Consider walk-in humidors for cigars, dedicated demonstration or learning spaces for in-store workshops, beer caves, root cellar-styled merchandising, more and larger fitting rooms, or experience zones for consumer electronics or video games. Focus on how your shoppers use the products you sell, then bring that experience into the store. Cabela's, REI and Williams Sonoma are known for doing this. Using the space to put your shoppers in the mind to buy may be as valuable as adding additional space.

Just as the largest stores are most likely to have lower space productivity, smaller stores are likely to have higher productivity. This is usually because the smallest stores tend to carry a narrow selection of only the best sellers in each category. Therefore, the issue facing the smallest stores is not about making them more productive, but about delivering an on-brand experience that isn't cluttered and trivial.

It's critical to recognize that not all businesses are equally important to your shoppers and that there is a minimum threshold that a business needs to attain in order for shoppers to consider making a purchase at your store. Consider greeting cards. If your "normal" selection of greeting cards is 40 linear feet, you probably carry a selection of birthday, wedding, graduation, anniversary and seasonal cards. A shopper who enters your store feels confident they can find a fitting card amongst your selection. But, if you had to reduce the greeting card section to only 8 linear feet, your shoppers may not find that selection to be worthwhile to shop. It doesn't meet their minimum viability criteria. So even though that 8 feet may contain your "best sellers" you could see the space productivity for that section decline below average because shoppers do not find your selection worthy.

Understanding the minimum viability for every business is key to improving the shopper experience for the smallest stores. There is a tendency to fit every single business line into the smallest stores even when it is only a half dozen of the best sellers from every category. That is when you get combination planograms that have Salad Dressing + Croutons + Mustards+ BBQ Sauce + Ketchup + Soy Sauce + Vinegar on one 4-foot section. At that point, the business needs to recognize that they have moved from being a grocery store to a convenience store and make more drastic cuts in entire business lines.

Moving from a full-selection store to a small footprint store by reducing entire categories sold in the store is usually accomplished by creating a sub-banner. Curated, small format stores usually have new names so that shoppers understand that they will not get the usual branded experience.

That leads to stores like the Walmart Neighborhood Market, Whole Foods Market Daily Shop, or Bloomingdale's Bloomies stores. What these national brands are doing is protecting their base brand store names by creating a sub-brand to signal to shoppers that they are not going to get the traditional full brand experience in the smaller format stores. But what is key to understand is that the smallest stores, by definition, cannot deliver the same product ranges and experiences so there must be determination to eliminate some business lines from the smallest stores. Space productivity combined with shopper insights can help each retailer determine when they have crossed a small store threshold and must start to eliminate businesses to meet their shopper's expectations.

So now that we have accounted for variances in the largest and the smallest stores, let's assume you have normalized the data for those outliers or eliminated them completely. Let's talk about the key elements to evaluate how to prioritize which stores have the most potential to improve if they were remodeled. What is most tricky about this analysis, is isolating a store's performance to the merchandising elements that can be changed during a remodel. Afterall, if the root cause of a store's performance is staff training, a swiftly changing neighborhood or natural disasters, remodeling the store cannot change that.

A power ranking of the stores that accounts for multiple measurements, is the most common way to evaluate stores across the fleet. The kinds of measurements that are useful in a power ranking come from more sources than space planning. They include:

- Revenue per square foot for the sales floor (eliminate the back room.) Include e-commerce sales if it is fulfilled by store inventory. Look at the percentage change year over year to see if the store is at or better than the chain's growth standard.
- The final dollar profit contribution per square foot for the sales floor

(eliminate the back room.) Include e-commerce sales if it is fulfilled by store inventory. Look at the percentage change year over year to see if the store is at or better than the chain's growth standard.

- The ratio of sales from key customer profiles. For example, the percent of sales from contractors versus DIYers, commercial sales, institutional sales, restaurants versus home cooks, etc. Look for variances that would explain significant business shifts for the store.

- The volume of online sales for the store's trading area when the e-commerce sales are fulfilled from a DC or direct from vendors. This helps identify shopping shifts that can cannibalize the local brick and mortar store's sales.

- Shrink from all sources: shoplifting, wastage, errors and fraud. Measuring shrink at the store level as well as the business line level can indicate businesses within the store that require relocation or new fixturing

- The out-of-stock rate for ongoing business lines as well as the sell through rate for seasonal goods. This can help identify when a store's lowered performance may be caused by a lack of inventory rather than a merchandising issue.

- The demographics for the area around the store as well as planned changes. The idea is to look for the right fit for the store before making major investments. If a retailer's target market is upscale, double income, no kids (DINK) households, it is important to learn if the surrounding trade area will soon have several hundred senior housing units open there in the coming years. Trade areas change over time and the ideal store is built for the market that is moving into a neighborhood.

- The overall evaluation score for the store manager on their most recent review. When evaluating stores against one another, it is erroneous to overlook the impact a store manager has on the store's performance.

- The store's Net Promoter Score. Customers review help validate the impact of the store on their behavior.

- The date of the last remodel or touchup effort in the store. An evaluation of the store's overall condition and aging. This can be and outcome based in the time since the store's last refresh but also the volume of customers served in high-traffic stores.

- Competition proximity. How close are your nearest competitors and have there been any store openings or closings that could explain your store's changing performance?

There are a lot of components to a high-quality power ranking. To make indexing store performance easier, some chains use a 5-star rating system to create an aggregate of the store's overall ranking.

Several times a year, executives should review the store power ranking to look for emerging trends. First, if there are stores that are pulling away and outperforming their cohorts, begin a root cause analysis to find out what is going right in those stores. Many chain-wide solutions come from grassroots efforts by store leaders. A combined operational and merchandising team can uncover what they are doing and try to extend their approach to other stores in the chain. Examples could include repositioning promotions in the store, community outreach efforts, an innovative stocking method or other tactics that are under the radar.

For those stores that are declining, look deeper into the greatest areas of opportunity. Use all the contributing measurements in the power ranking report to uncover root causes. Again, deploy a combined operational and merchandising team to audit stores in decline to look for commonalities. If there is a common issue, create a program to address it. A new SOP and locking fixture might deter shoplifting, extending store hours during key holidays may capture more market share, or improving promotional forecasting may properly balance allocated inventory to the right stores. Your research can go many ways. Only one of which is a need to remodel a store.

In the case where a remodel seems to be the right move, carefully weigh the cost of disrupting the store and its shoppers. Even when stores are improved, there will be weeks or months of disrupted shopping patterns. If the store improvement is fractional, it may be worth postponing the investment to another time when the ROI will be higher.

Execution & Compliance – Mastering The Operations

O ur well-thought-out space plans are meant to delight our shoppers and make our stores easier to operate. But the plans can only work if they are executed and maintained. It is incredibly rewarding to see a section that is well merchandised and exactly as you intended it being shopped by customers in the stores. But there is plenty that needs to happen between the time you hit "publish" until the store looks the way it was designed.

Yet in an AMR study, retailers said they estimated that only 59% execute their merchandising and promotion initiatives as intended.[8] Usually, there are two main culprits: communication and labor hours to complete the tasks. As a space planner, you may not be able to influence the labor budget component, but effective, timely communication is in your control.

First, why does it matter that your stores look the way they were planned? It matters for both your shoppers and your company's financial success. Store resets and planogram changes are created to deliver the most current and attractive selections to your shoppers.

If you hear the term "speed to market," it means that your operation is

---

[8]   Source: supermarketnews.com/technology/getting-things-done

streamlined so that you can get new products on shelves and into the market faster than your competition. That matters because brands usually spend most of their marketing money on new product launches. Advertising, promotional offers and special prices help push a new product into the shoppers' minds and disrupt their usual shopping patterns. If your stores are late to put those new products onto the shelves, you miss the power of all that marketing investment. Plus, your shoppers may have discovered those new items elsewhere and satisfied their curiosity there. As a shopping destination, you want your stores to be current and up to date. Showcasing new items gives your overall banner a halo of being a modern place that reliably keeps up with trends and new offerings.

Your category financial plans also require fast, reliable execution to get new offerings in the stores. Let's say there is a department that is declining slightly. Maybe sales are down -2% versus the previous year. But there is a new refresh for the entire aisle and with the change in space and a stronger offering, your company expect sales to change to a +5% trajectory. Slow movers are being discontinued. Hot new items are introduced. There's new signs and a new online presence to announce the changes. If there is even a two-week delay in the execution, the chances of meeting the company's financial goals are in jeopardy. Because instead of improved sales starting in the first week, the department continues its downward sales decline for another two weeks. Now 50 weeks of sales needs to reverse sales that were forecasted to change over 52 weeks. Which means the change must be even more successful than was planned. That is a lot of additional pressure to put on a merchandising change that could have been avoided if the execution had just occurred when it was scheduled.

So proper execution that is done with speed and as planned is important. It isn't just "change for change's sake." It keeps your store fresh, interesting to shoppers and improves sales by leaning into supplier marketing campaigns for new items.

It is also the culmination of months of strategic and financial planning. That planning involves all the activities that go into creating a planogram. This includes assortment plan and macro space allocation, working with suppliers, setting up item data, selecting the final assortment, capturing updated store-layouts and new fixtures, and building and reviewing planograms with Category Managers. Then we can finally launch into execution and all that it implies. There are all of the corporate and supply chain activities as well as store activities to convert digital planograms into store realities. It includes writing up the orders and ramping up inventory so it arrives on time, marking down discontinued items, coordinating the communication to the stores, scheduling the hours to complete the work and finally, making the physical changes at the shelf. If the plan cannot be reliably executed, then the effort and resources that went into the plan development was squandered. All the work comes down to getting the execution right.

Preparing the Change

It helps to know who will do the changes in the stores. Will it be retailer employees? Are they merchandising specialists? Or will it be whomever is assigned the task? Will it be a third-party team that comes into the store to execute the change? Will vendors assist or even be responsible for the change? Will it happen during normal business hours or overnight? Who will supervise and verify the work is completed?

All of this matters because each of those groups may have different resources and responsibilities while they are executing the changes. For example, if it is the retailer team, understanding union requirements can impact everything from the hours and number of people assigned to the merchandising change to the weight of the fixtures and product that is merchandised. Different teams may have different access to the tools they need to complete the job as well.

In any case, a test run before the change is deployed is a good idea. Many retailers have an innovation center or a store prototype that is not on the market that serves as their experimentation store. Merchants, vendors and space planners can collaborate in a physical "store" to review the change, approve it or make changes before it is distributed across the chain. These laboratory stores have their own operational challenges managing inventory and scheduling. But for retailers with the resources to have an innovation store, they can prevent problems and misalignments before they happen. As more execution teams rely on video instructions, the innovation stores are also exemplary demonstration studios where fixture changes, merchandising instructions and display building can be recorded and edited before going out into the field.

With an internal or external team, they need to be able to access the planogram and floorplan directions. Usually, this is considered a store asset, and access is controlled through a store email or store device. If it is being sent to an external team, there are protocols for ensuring that the correct team can access their assigned store's instructions. It is a best practice to access the change documents and review them prior to the actual reset event. That allows teams to assess the scope of the change and consider an approach that will be least disruptive to shoppers or other operational activities that will be happening in the store at the same time.

Here are the usual materials provided in a planogram change:

- New Planogram – full set and each section on a separate page.
- Line Listing – a report of the products on each location with facings, orientation and shelf capacity.
- Fixture Bill of Materials (BOM) – a listing of all the fixtures required to make the change.
- Fixture Position – a way to see exactly where each fixture should be positioned prior to merchandising it. (May be integrated with the sectional view of the planogram.)

- Disposition/Discontinued Report – the items that will be removed and not remerchandised in the new setup.
- An estimate for the amount of time to complete the change.

Additional optional materials:

- What's Changed – key elements to note in the change.
- New Product Information – features and benefits for customers to help when engaging with customers.
- Current planogram – for comparison.
- Performance reports – highlighting the best sellers.

Most teams will print out the new planogram by section at a minimum. While most modern planogramming solutions offer a store-facing module that provides all these materials to a mobile device, most stores use the sectional view to assist with the change during the reset. (See more on this later.*) If stores print all or some portion of the final instructions at the store, most retailers provide .PDF versions of the final output. PDF is a universally accepted format that can reliably reproduce the graphical elements of a planogram without distortion. While many retailers are making a shift to a completely digital planograms using hand-held devices to access them in the stores, PDF as an output still predominates.

Floor plan changes have similar materials to support them. The teams that are required to make a floorplan swap can be minimal. Like when one category is losing space to an adjacent category that is gaining the same space. Or they can require teams of people. Like the transformational changes when aisles and departments are reconfigured, power and ceiling plans change, and new fixtures are constructed in the store. Depending on the changes, materials that get sent to support a floor plan change could include:

- New Floor Plan – perhaps with just the changed area isolated for large stores.

- Old Floor Plan – for comparison.
- Fixture Bill of Materials (BOM) – a listing of all the macro fixtures required to make the change.
- Disposition Directions – what to do with any fixtures or signs coming off the sale floor.

Additional Optional Materials:

- Electrical plan – for electrician and inspection.
- Sign Placement Direction – for overhead and permanent signs.
- Building permits – where necessary.
- Display building plans – if there are larger-scale displays to be set up.
- Resource contacts – how to reach the project manager for issue escalation.
- Renderings and 3-D Views – elevation plans to help visualize the outcome.

For store teams to have time to prepare, ideally there is at least 2 weeks for a planogram and 2 months for a major floor plan change that requires trades and outside resources. This allows for situations in stores where the responsible leader creates schedule accommodations the week prior to the reset. Or if there are local resources that need to be scheduled like storage containers or extra dumpsters that the store needs to arrange.

Finally, let's be clear that not every organization or every business has their needs best addressed through a planogram. Some businesses are merchandised with look books and recommended merchandising schemes that merchandisers in the stores use as guides for their presentations. For example, in those stores that have high churn in a seasonal or apparel area and a diverse set of merchandising conditions in the stores, it may be best to provide a series of photos that illustrate acceptable options for merchandise presentation based on the selection, inventory levels and display fixtures that each store has. A seasonal Halloween apparel display is showcased differently if one store has access to mannequins and hanging racks while another has nesting tables and acrylic stands. Photos that show how to best display their likely selection in multiple configurations can serve as visual direction for merchandisers who work in the store. This is a common approach for home décor, furnishings, apparel and seasonal products.

For retailers who follow a "look book" or plan-o-guide approach to some business lines, it is important to have strong merchandising talent working in the stores. Build district and regional merchandising experts to work with store team to instruct, inspect and improve merchandising in every store. Include important materials and guidance along with photos so that the store merchandisers understand the themes of the presentation and the key anchor items in the range. Priority lists are very helpful.

Retailers who commonly use the "look book" approach and then rely on strong in-store merchandisers include furniture stores, home furnishings, clothing boutiques and art galleries. In most cases, the in-store merchandising team has full rein to decide where and how products in their store will be merchandised.

Sitting between the "look book" approach and the fully planogrammed merchandising schemes is directed merchandising. With directed merchandising, the stores are given direction about where products are to be placed in their store. But the merchandisers use the inventory and fixtures to make the best presentation possible. Examples of this directed merchandising includes grocery bakery and produce departments. Stores will have specific citrus tables or pie tables, but the store personnel determine the best way to present their inventory to their shoppers. This is a common approach for apparel chain stores, floral departments, plant nurseries, jewelry cases and footwear departments.

When a retailer uses a look book or directed merchandising strategy, it is important that stores are given clear communication about expected sales plans and priorities. That way the in-store team can ensure that they are placing the most important products in the most visible locations and that there is enough space for the expected inventory deliveries. Space teams or visual merchandising teams rely on strong communicators in corporate roles to interpret the merchant plans into photos and directions to support those areas. They must be up to date on the prevalent store conditions and sell through rates in order to produce clear communication about when to relocate products, where to use signs and how to efficiently provide direction to stores.

Making the Change

Good merchandising hygiene begins with the habitual practice of following the same procedure to deliver consistent outcomes. Retail operators know that usually means a checklist.

A planogram change checklist:

- Print Planograms by section*.
- Print new price tags for the planogram.
- Remove all discontinued items and segregate them into their own carts. Either return to vendor (RTV), destroy or move to clearance markdown location(s) as directed in the disposition.
- Remove all products. Best practice: place each brand in its own car to make remerchandising easier.
- Stage new items for the planogram at or near the aisle from the back room.
- Tape planogram section printouts to the backboard of every section.
- Clean all fixtures. Wash shelves.
- Place fixture to their proper locations prior to remerchandising.
- Place 1 unit for each facing to replicate the new planogram.
- Review against the planogram. Have someone verify and approve that

locations are accurate.
- Place new price labels in for each item.
- Fill facings with available inventory to complete the planogram.
- Place any promotional or temporary signs in place.
- Final store manager/department manager walk through and approval.
- Compliance report to HQ (with photos if required.)

From the store's point of view, it is a good practice to track and report the actual reset time for future forecast improvements. If the reset could not be completed as planned, note the reasons. Typical reasons include product did not arrive in time (hold the space for the new item on the set), missing fixtures, broken fixtures, missing signs, incorrect planogram match to space available (should identify in preparation phase – not on the date of execution.)

From the headquarters' point of view, there are things that can help support a successful change in every store. First, in the weeks leading up to the change, track and monitor new fixture deliveries. Each store should have their new fixtures a week or more before the reset so that mis-shipments or lost-in-transit fixtures can be addressed before the reset date. Your fixture vendors can assist by labeling the outside of all boxes to stores "Fixture pkg for reset week of October 1" or "Support materials for Project 9728. Box 1 of 7." The boxes should be identifiable at the receiving dock.

If you have project readiness reporting, you can be prepared to make adjustments before impacting customer experience. Project readiness reporting includes critical process metrics that track the elements required to succeed. Your project readiness could include the planogram publish date, the new item order date, new items received at the DC, store labor hours allocated (or third-party labor notified), new fixtures orders, new fixtures shipped and received, new signs printed, new signs shipped and received, etc. In other words, there should be a way to track at a macro level how the chain is prepared for the transition and drill down capabilities to understand individual issues for stores or components. A project readiness report is the kind of KPI (Key Performance Indicator) that is actionable because it predicts success instead of evaluating success (or failure) after an event.

You can also evaluate new item readiness with similar reporting for all new items added to a reset. Report on the % of stores that had received the new items by the date of the reset. This should be a standard report that Category and Inventory Managers can access the weeks leading up to a reset. Any gaps can be addressed with either distributors or vendors.

Once the planogram has executed, be prepared to produce a standard planogram success scorecard for each reset. Items you can consider in that scorecard include:

- % of stores successfully implementing the change +/- X days of the plan.
- Sales for the XX weeks before the reset versus XX weeks after the reset.
- Labor spent versus labor planned to complete the reset.
- Common issues or problems cited in store feedback.
- Issues addressed in reset.

Then, follow up the reset in 3 months with a first quarter performance review. The review should measure the performance against the elements that were identified in the strategic meeting (reduce out of stocks for XYZ or improve margin for ABC.) You can also track performance by set size or store cluster. If possible, use market data to compare category share of wallet pre- and post-implementation. This is a crucial point in the category plan process. If the plan is delivering the benefits as expected, then the annual category plan can proceed. If it is falling short, the CM and supporting teams can decide which adjustments to make. Not all adjustments have to impact the planogram. CM's have more reactionary levers at their disposal by changing pricing, promotions and possibly restructuring deals with vendors.

To build trust and transparency, sharing topline benefits with store management and operators can help them connect the work they complete in the store with the results. Afterall, they probably have sales goals and quotas to meet themselves. So, it is in the best interest of everyone to have as much clarity around how store efforts are paying off (or not) as possible. Making sure your store teams have access to this crucial piece of communication helps build teamwork and provides purpose.

Monitoring & Maintaining the Change

Planogram compliance – indeed all merchandising execution compliance in stores – provides a wealth of information that can provide operational insights. Generally, planogram compliance is meant to evaluate the difference between the store-level reality after a planogram change versus the intended planned presentation in that store.

A true picture of the store's reality is the foundation for a retailer's item location effort. Item location is the ability of a customer or store employee to find the exact location for any item in the store. The data that is gathered during planogram compliance can be placed in a real-time database for a customer-facing app or internal inventory locations. It can also improve shelf availability when it is integrated to replenishment models and cycle counting. The compliance monitoring can become a source of truth for many downstream systems and analysis.

Planogram compliance can happen at any time. But generally, it is most critical when initially completing the planogram revision (Day One.) Day One compliance monitoring evaluates whether the store was set up as planned for the initial presentation. It is valuable since it typically identifies physical obstacles or late deliveries of new items that can be immediately resolved. This is especially important if third party merchandising staff is still in the store and can address the issues.

Planogram compliance is a journey. It delivers improved benefits as it evolves. Consider these various definitions of planogram compliance:

Space analytics Is a primary advocate for planogram compliance since it improves space productivity measurements. Store operators can also benefit when they are responsible for picking customer curbside orders or when locating merchandise for customers.

To implement planogram compliance, the store needs to have a particular planogram assigned to its category. "Planoguides" and situations where a store selects the planogram that most reflects its conditions cannot be used for compliance monitoring. Also, if planograms do not allocate space for local items, stores will regularly fail to meet 100% compliance. Many retailers find it difficult to deliver compliance metrics for areas like produce, meat, seafood, apparel, floral and prepared foods areas where they use directed merchandising instead of planograms.

For retailers who are serious about compliance, there are many possible solutions. At the highest level, the shelf is compared to the planogram database to uncover exceptions. Feedback can be in real time or provided in reports to both the store and relevant support functions (space planning, replenishment, store operations, etc.) The compliance comparison and feedback remain the same and is customized by each retailer. What changes is the method for gathering the scan of the in-store conditions.

Store associates themselves or a service provider in the store can scan items at the shelf using a hand-held device. Using image recognition (IR) software, employees can take photos of the completed sections. The photos are translated into data that is compared to the planogram files to find compliance issues. Rather than use employees, robots can cycle through the store and take photos to gather the planogram condition. Fixed cameras on shelves or set into the ceiling can constantly surveil the shelf conditions and watch shopper patterns. An adaptation of that is to use cameras that move by either rotating or sliding along tracks.

Image recognition has come a long way since it began being used ~2009 for shelf compliance. There is an ongoing struggle with items like toothbrushes, lipsticks, apparel and undifferentiated small items. But on the whole, the technology has evolved and is a reliable tool for space planners to leverage to access in store conditions. IR reporting can validate proof of performance when brands have paid for a specific store position, the placement of point-of-sale material and new item cut-ins. It can also alert store operators or replenishment systems when out of stocks are recognized.

This summary from Georges Mirza: *Innovating Category Management* is a great framework:

Function	Hand-Held	Robots	Fixed Camera	Semi-Fixed Camera
Planogram Compliance	Y	Y	Y	Y
Stock Condition (OOS, Low, Medium, instock)	Y	Y	Y	Y
Price Tag Present	Y	Y	Y	Y
Shelf Tag Matches Product	Limited	Y	Limited	Limited
Barcode Detection	Limited	Y	Limited	Limited
Video Capture	Y	Y	N	Y
Overstock	Y	N	Y	Y
Product Image (Gathering & Recognition)	Medium	Medium	High	High
Shopper Disruption	Medium	High	Low/NA	Low/NA
Cost	Low	High	Medium	Low
Install/ Implementation Cost	Low/NA	Medium	High	Low
Maintenance Needs	Low/NA	High	Medium	Low
Human Dependency	High	Medium	Medium	Low
Scan Frequency (per day)	Labor Availability	1-3	Unlimited	Unlimited
Near Real Time	Labor Availability	N	Y	Y
Safety Concerns	NA	Medium	NA	NA

As you can see, a lot can be discovered by monitoring planogram compliance. A real-world example happened when a store missed its sales goals on large, bagged rice. Those big bags were merchandised on the bottom shelf. Image recognition (from a robot, shelf-mount or human) identified that while the bags are present, all the tags on the bottom shelf were missing. Seems the floor cleaning machine the night crew used knocked them off the bottom shelf. Since shoppers do not purchase items when they don't know the price, the sales were down the next day. Any other system would have said the items were in stock so there would not be a flag to store personnel to monitor the situation. But IR could quickly identify the issue and create a job ticket for store team members to re-print the tags and place them on the shelf.

Why all this focus on exactly following a planogram? (i.e. planogram compliance.)

First, most retailers plan their initial inventory allocation and replenishment minimum orders to fill the shelf as designed in the planogram. If the merchandising is executed with more or less facings than planned, the inventory will not fit or be too thin to stretch across the shelf. If stores can reliably execute planograms, initial order quantities based on planograms can be accurately forecasted and ordered using automation.

Second, many retailers make shelf placement promises to their suppliers. In some cases, suppliers pay a premium or extend a special merchandising fund to guarantee prime placement. In order to collect the fund and prove the placement was executed, retailers must have a way to capture the planogram conditions in the store.

Third, to evaluate the productivity of products and merchandising placements, retailers and their suppliers may rely on the planogram as a version of the truth. For example, let's say Brand A is selling at $52.50 per linear foot and Brand B is selling at $37.80 per linear foot. We could improve our space productivity and satisfy more customers by trading space away from

Brand B and toward Brand A. But we cannot make that decision, unless we are confident that we know exactly how much space Brand A and Brand B have on the store shelves. Extend this analogy from brands to subcategories, categories and even departments and you can see why space analysis and space productivity improvements require accurate space awareness of how products were truly merchandised and not just how they were planned to be merchandised.

Planogram degradation over time is a real issue that needs to be considered beyond Day One compliance measurements. As items are replenished and shopper patterns impact the presentation, products can shift. This is especially true if the planogram did not account for a minimum case pack requirement for each item. Depending on your restocking frequency and shopper traffic, planograms can degrade in less than 30 days. Meaning that the merchandising integrity falls to such a point that the original (Day One) scans are invalid.

To address planogram degradation, retailers have several options. They can scan shelves more frequently and provide store operators with metrics and direction to address the changes. This is easily accomplished if the retailer is using robots or mounted cameras. They can have more frequent planogram maintenance tasks added to the store team's labor allocation. They can have frequent "minor planogram tweaks" on a regular basis that requires the stores to meet "day one" merchandising accuracy. Perhaps one of the most powerful tactics for maintaining planogram integrity is to make planogram reviews a part of every district or regional manager's visit. Naturally, they do not have to review each planogram. But reviewing a random sampling of planograms against the current standards and plan will help store team members focus on planogram execution year-round.

Maybe you are wondering what "good" planogram compliance is? What is the gold standard you should set for your organization? Consider this: planogram compliance is a spectrum that needs to be as good as your company requires it to be. If your company uses planograms to create item location in the stores for online order picking or for customer convenience, then your planogram compliance needs to be very high. At least to the section/shelf level. If your company scans the shelves using robots or some other means to create the data for item location, then planogram compliance may not need to be so high. Amazon's just walk out stores required nearly 100% planogram compliance so that every item in the store had a single home location. But a mom-and-pop franchise store may not need anywhere near that kind of adherence to corporate merchandising to succeed.

If your company uses planograms to set ordering quantities or to allocate products to new stores, you need planogram compliance to the shelf/facing level. Stores will receive inventory that will fit if they set the planogram exactly as planned. Otherwise, they will struggle to have home locations for the products and quantities they receive.

Most companies expect planogram compliance in the 90th percentiles. But many companies fall far below that.

How to improve planogram compliance

To begin, your team can ensure that the right planograms are assigned to the correct stores. Stores have a legitimate complaint if they have an assigned planogram that is not proper for their store conditions. Begin with the "right fit." Which means that the planogram must have the correct dimensions for the store's fixtures so that the items in the store can fit on the shelves as the planogram directs.

Then, the right assortment and inventory needs to be allocated to the store. That usually means a direct connection between the planogram and the inventory systems so that the planogram can authorize items for distribution and the planogram facings can generate the current quantity allocation. That inventory needs to arrive at the store in time for the scheduled reset. That is especially key if the store is serviced by an outside agency that is responsible for planogram resets. If the product arrives late, there is a strong possibility that it will not be merchandised correctly. Exception reports that highlight products on a planogram but not in the store's inventory on the day of the reset can provide insight into this compliance blocker.

Once you are certain that the correct planogram and inventory are reaching the stores in time, the next step to POG compliance is ensuring that the store teams have the hours available to execute the planogram on time. Most companies evaluate planogram changes based on their complexity and size to arrive at an estimate for store labor. And it adds up quickly! Something as simple as a 15 minute one-for one swap for a handful of items can cost $60,000 if 800 stores execute that change. Those additional tasks and costs cannot just be "absorbed" by the normal store labor budget. The stores need the budget and the staff availability to execute the change. Usually, this is negotiated and planned months in advance of the change.

The team members in the stores must have both access to the new planogram and training on how to use the planogram materials. Access can be as cumbersome as getting to a computer in the store office, logging in, navigating to the proper folder, downloading the planogram PDF packet, printing it and taking it to the store floor. Or it can be available on a hand-held mobile device. But in either case, there has to be a recipient in the store that knows how to access the planogram packet.

Reading planograms are not second nature to most people. Your full-time space planners may be perfectly comfortable with the front-view, side-view, discontinued list and line listing. But for a new store employee, just navigating the packet and reports can be overwhelming. Especially if they only receive a new planogram. Understanding what does and does not change from their current merchandising requires orientation and familiarity with the products on the shelf and in the planogram. Some companies help to overcome this barrier by using full color images of the products. But even that may not help if the product packaging is small. Others use tools like One Door Store Assistant™ or MerchLogix's Navigator™ to convert planograms into task-based instructions. This is super-critical when the work of changing a planogram is handed off from one employee to another.

Then, one must assume that the store team is able to make the planogram change itself. That they have the necessary fixturing, displays, baskets, peg hooks, hangers and any other element used in the planogram. Using a before/after fixture report can highlight any additional fixtures that store team members need to acquire from the fixture back room. Or new fixtures that need to be purchased and sent to the store.

All of this is BEFORE the planogram is even touched.

Let's assume all of these items have been addressed. To improve planogram compliance, first you must measure and baseline compliance. As we discussed earlier, measurement can occur at multiple levels (see the Granularity Table earlier in the chapter.) Amongst the ways that planogram compliance gets measured is:

1. A yes/no check box by the store themselves to say they completed the planogram. A "yes" infers that the POG was completed in full. The planogram may or may not be reviewed by s store manager or department leader.
2. A yes/no check box plus a photo uploaded by the store to indicate the job was done. The photo can be manually referenced, if necessary, by corporate or multi-unit leaders.
3. A photo uploaded to an image recognition engine that compares the photo to the expected planogram. The system then flags any changes for the store or the store team members can explain why they cannot rectify a problem.

Store Reviews where store conditions are compared to planograms are powerful planogram compliance reinforcing tactics. When a store manager, district manager or regional merchandising manager reviews a store and includes planogram compliance in the store evaluation, it raises planogram execution to the same levels as loss prevention, inventory management and labor scheduling.

Since planogram compliance relies on so many other areas to succeed, elevating planogram compliance KPI's to other dashboards can improve outcomes. Consider a measurement for store allocators that would measure the number of items on planogram that were not in store on the date of the expected reset. A similar measurement cold be created to track whether new fixtures and signs arrived on time. Even planograms must be completed on time to set stores up for success. Providing critical KPI's on POG compliance to category managers gives them the ability to see root causes for sales forecast variations.

Space Planning Teams - Mastering The Organization

T here is no perfect space planning team design that works for every situation. Each company will customize the roles, organization and resources differently depending on the company's size, systems, processes and strategy. This chapter will consider the roles within a company that ought to be considered when creating or overhauling a space planning capability. These will vary depending on whether the space planning function supports a retailer or a consumer brand in service of its retail customers. But in any case, the space planning organization needs to be designed to facilitate clear cross-functional communication, fast processing and a laser focus on shopper satisfaction.

The Space Team in Consumer Brands

For consumer brands, space planning capabilities typically reside within the Category Management practice that supports customers with assortment planning, pricing analysis, shopper insights and other key category management levers. It is not unusual for space planning to be one of many disciplines that a category management partner will practice in the course of supporting a key retail customer. Thus, they will conduct a syndicated data market share analysis one week, a competitive price shop analysis the next and produce several dozen planograms the next. For consumer brands, the question of where to place the space practice is fairly easy: it is part of a sales support function that has a goal of increasing customer partnership and relationships through trusted advice.

How deeply the space and category management functions are divided from sales operations (with their quotas and volume goals) will be up to each organization. Some companies deliberately organize the category management function within a market support team that only indirectly interfaces with salespeople. Their work is assigned and evaluated apart from each retail customer's volume goal. But that is rare. Most brands embed the category management support functions within a multi-disciplined retail team that is organized around providing the best support possible to match up to a retailer's internal team. Thus, a brand supply chain team member is aligned to the retailer's supply chain team. The shopper insights researcher is paired up to the retailer's marketing insights team. And the space planning resource is paired up with the retailer's merchandising and presentation team. The depth and frequency of the interactions between the brand and the retailer teams is a result of the companies' sizes, the influence of each company on one another's goals and the shared commitment they have made to working together.

There are a variety of ways that brands support their retail customers that range from the most trusted and intimate to a merely transactional encounter. Some brands have their space resources co-located within the retailer's offices to support daily interactions. Usually, those situations occur where the brand spans many of the retailer's categories. Some brands only interface annually with the buying team to recommend and influence merchandising strategies.

Because brands are typically limited to influencing planograms and micro-space, it is rare for consumer brands to support a macro space function. Some large CPGs may be able to influence macro space within a single aisle like the laundry aisle, the cereal aisle or the paint and stain aisle. But while they may recommend space allocation swaps between hot and cold cereal, for example, they are not empowered to make the changes or analyze the entire store in the way that a retailer's team can.

Nevertheless, while a brand's space resources are absolved from dealing with the retailer's complexity of floor planning and macro space analysis, they are saddled with supporting many different planogram systems. Since retailers require that planogram files integrate seamlessly with their internal systems, brands may find that they have to support half a dozen different space planning systems across their entire customer portfolio. This causes overhead costs for the brands. To that end, many convert their retail customer's files to a system of choice, execute the changes in their preferred system and then convert the files back to the retailer's criteria. Out of legacy decisions, most retailers and their suppliers have selected the .PSA (Blue Yonder) data file as the standard planogram file format. So that means that brands may have to take a non-.PSA file into their system, convert it to a PSA file, edit that file, export the .PSA file and then the retailer must convert and ingest it back into their system. Not a very streamlined process.

One of the exciting promises of SAAS, cloud-based space solutions is the promise of allowing brand space support teams to access the retailer's own space solution instance and work directly in the same system that the retailer natively uses. With user access permissions controlled by the retailer, single sign on and multi-factor authentication routines, the retailer can control the data access and change permissions for their vendor partners. This will reduce the time and effort to convert data files on both sides. Retailer-created validations can be enforced, and joint planogram production can be more collaborative. Once widely adopted, brands can eliminate the multiple POG systems they currently support and license. The end-to-end system will be more efficient and less expensive.

For a consumer brand to be especially effective, it is important that they have a robust category library. Whereas a retailer can be satisfied with a subset of all the products in a category and their relevant attributes for their market, a consumer brand who supports many retailers needs to have a category library that is comprehensive. Not only should it contain every possible product available for the market (or nation!), but it should also contain deeply specific attribution.

For example, a retailer may only be able to scratch the surface of their pet food assortment by attributing an item as Cat or Dog and Wet or Dry. A brand should carry much deeper data elements to help a retailer analyze their merchandise assortment and presentation based on cat vs dog, puppy/kitten /adult/aging pet, single or multiple animal households, dietary needs, price segmentation, ingredient components, nutritional value per pound, national ad spend, coupon and aggregator activity by market, packaging recyclability, fair trade sourcing, etc. There are many different ways that a retailer and their partner will want to evaluate their presentation and assortment. Which means different analyses need to be anticipated with complete data so that the consumer brand partner can be as supportive as possible.

When resourcing a space support team, consider creating a team that is comprised of career category management experts who lead the practice. They are the thought leaders who can set the team strategy, resourcing and planning. They should be well-respected amongst their peers and capable of making ethical decisions when there are conflicting objectives between sales leaders and retail customers. Augment their staff with a regular rotation of sales resources who will be placed in a category management role for rotations of 2+ years. The goal of the rotation is full exposure to category management practices which will make them more capable retail partners with their future accounts. They will understand and appreciate the work that is required to create objective category plans. And they will be more thoughtful partners when collaborating with internal and external teams.

The Space Team in Retailers

For retailers, the space team is not always found within the same functional area. Some retailers see the outcome of a space planning team as being "the last yard of the supply chain" and, thus, the space planning team is within the supply chain and inventory planning pyramid. Others see it as a tactical element of the category management process and in those cases, the space planning team reports into the merchandising silo. Some retailers believe that the space planning team and its work is tightly tied to the retail operations teams in the stores and their tasks. So those retailers have the space planning team report into retail operations executives. Finally, there is a scattering of other organizational designs where space planning may report. Some report to the Chief Marketing Officer (where the "brand" element of merchandising is the focus.) Some report into the Real Estate and Construction area. Especially if the macro and micro space planning teams are separated. It speaks to the multifunctional impact of Space Planning that there is such a diversity of organizations.

Ultimately, there is not a "right" place for space planning. There are pros and cons to every reporting strategy. The important thing is to understand how the retailer views and values space planning and to deliver against that.

Nevertheless, it is most common to find the micro space planning team to be very closely aligned to category managers and the merchandising function. The macro space planning team is nearly always tightly connected to the real estate and construction teams. Even if they do not formally report to those areas.

Other functions that may be included within a space team include the space operations and administration function which manages the systems, training and processes that the space operators use. The fixture planning team that procures and catalogs all fixtures in the stores. The space analytics team (more about that below.) The sign teams which may be responsible for permanent, temporary, sale and price signs in the stores and the tactical systems that create those signs. Visual merchandising and display resources that create custom presentations for store execution. GNFR (Goods Not For Resale) planning and replenishment teams which may include elements for new stores (like ladders, trash bins, floor mats, stools) as well as consumable products that stores require (like register tape, pens, bags and PLU stock.) Store communications teams that aggregate all messages from multiple areas for direct communications to stores. Finally, if the retailer has its own merchandising resources in the field, they may also report into the space planning leader – giving that leader end-to-end responsibility for merchandising planning and execution in the stores.

Again, every retailer will manage their resources differently. But here is a way to think about how retailers may expand or contract their space planning department into other areas when devising their organizational structure.

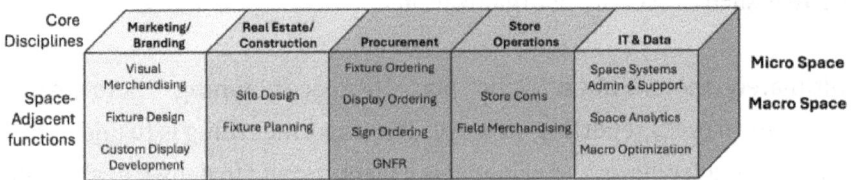

Core Disciplines	Marketing/ Branding	Real Estate/ Construction	Procurement	Store Operations	IT & Data	
Space-Adjacent functions	Visual Merchandising	Site Design	Fixture Ordering	Store Coms	Space Systems Admin & Support	Micro Space
	Fixture Design	Fixture Planning	Display Ordering	Field Merchandising	Space Analytics	Macro Space
	Custom Display Development		Sign Ordering		Macro Optimization	
			GNFR			

Figure 22: Space Adjacent functions which may be embedded in a retailer's space planning team.

When a retailer seeds their space planning team, it is ideal to have a balance of past experiences and skill sets. Experience in executing major reset changes and planogram transitions is always in demand. Many space planning leaders follow the maxim "Give me a great merchandiser and I can teach them a system. But I cannot teach a systems operator to be a great merchandiser." But be clear: much of the day for a space planner is primarily with a computer.

Which means if a field merchandiser gets their energy source from the physical demands and customer interactions that happen in a store, they may be very stifled by being in a space planning department.

Other skill sets that make for a balanced team are experience in merchandising and item set up, data analysis, store labor planning and communications, architectural design, visual merchandising, promotional or inventory planning and database administration. A balance of people from the retailer's own store as well as competitors can bring in fresh approaches and solutions. As with CPG's, a rotation in the space planning department can improve a merchant, inventory planner or store leader's understanding of how space works. Space positions that are regularly staffed as part of an identified career development plan can make a stronger merchandising team over time.

Within micro space there is an ongoing debate over whether space team members should report into the space team or the category team that they support. When space planners support a diverse set of categories, this is not contested. The space leader is their leader. But if a space planner is monopolized by one business line (like frozen foods or hand tools) then the retailer must consider the benefits of having space resources embedded within category teams.

First, there is the opportunity to align all compensation plans. If there are bonuses for attaining category goals, then having space team members participate in those compensation plans can motivate all support members to drive for the same outcomes. That applies to inventory replenishment, forecasting, promotions and all other support resources that work on a category's business. Second, it allows for better decision making through deeper participation in the business by the space planner. When a space planner is engaged in strategic plans and vendor presentations, they can be more adept at making the correct merchandising decisions when faced with display challenges and will not need to seek guidance from the category managers so frequently. Third, it creates the right focus for all supporting team members so that driving sales and shopper satisfaction always usurps individual functional goals that can sometimes dilute focus.

Whether or not a retailer chooses to formally align space resources with specific category teams, it is critical that space team members forge strong communication lines with their merchant partners. Space team members who merely check in with their buying partners once a year to get an updated assortment list and execute the changes to the planograms, miss out on developing deep understanding of the category and its shoppers. Knowing shopper behavior and how they shop is what helps a space planner make the best presentation decisions possible when creating planograms. Space planners should ask to participate in strategic shopper insight sessions and should ask for new product positioning materials so that they can provide the best chance possible for every product in an assortment to succeed in stores.

Space systems are so unique and have such complicated administration that it is common to have an administrative "super user" embedded within the space planning team. Some retailers have several people who play this role and together they manage ongoing release upgrades, onboarding and training, user authentication and permissions, new capability development, process management and trouble shooting. Because the use of the space system is so closely aligned to the department's success, it is unusual to have those resources embedded in the IT team. Business users and the system administrators are sometimes in daily communication to ensure that job packages and system configurations stay synchronized. For those roles, a DBA (data base administrator) and someone who knows simple code languages (java, SQL, VB) can make a multiplier impact on the overall team's productivity. Increasingly, retailers rely on scripting and custom batch jobs to scale space productivity across the enterprise.

Space team leaders are as unique as the teams they lead. But the watch word for every retailer space team is accuracy. Since the work of a space team can impact thousands of actions in the stores, it is critical that every single fixture or product placement is accurate. Space team leaders always focus on quality, accuracy and timeliness.

In some retailers, the space team is a tactical team that implements plans that are given to them. The space leader must understand how to motivate their team to deliver high quality, consistent work every single week. They focus on recognition, skill development and production delivery. Adherence to a process that produces reliable results is nonnegotiable.

Other retailers imbue the space team with more creativity and accountability for merchandise presentation in the stores. For those retailers, space team leaders need to have a deep understanding of how the retail brand and their shoppers' experience is augmented by merchandising. Their singular focus is usually on how the merchandising plans come to life in the store and whether or not shoppers respond to each distinctive presentation.

For people who want to build a career in space planning, the most important element is to be a trusted partner across many different functions. A space leader is a critical partner for merchants, store managers, inventory planning, store construction, real estate, financial planning and marketing. A space team leader must be able to navigate multiple priorities and reconcile company goals that are in opposition. Developing communication skills is critical – but communicating well does not surpass the need to be a trusted partner. Space team leaders will often find themselves delivering news that the audience doesn't want to hear. Because they understand the limitations of store teams, the supply chain and financial obstacles, they will regularly be in the position to bring strategic dreams down to reality. The temptation will be high to tell the audience what they want to hear. But if you cannot deliver on those promises, trust in your personal brand will fade quickly. If you can develop a reputation for being a fair and flexible person who sees every commitment through, you will succeed.

Where Does Analytics Belong?

Space analytics measures the productivity of store space with a goal of improving the return on the retailer's real estate investment. Space planners have the ability to make merchandising changes to improve shelf availability, positioning within the store, space allocation, adjacencies or improved shop-ability. Space analytics are meant to measure the production of store space and indicate how to make those improvements so that every store is selling as much as possible and is meeting its shopper's expectations.

The measurements can range from the simplistic (sales per square foot – available through any retailer's tax filings) to the sophisticated (marginal gross margin return on space based on direct product profitability inclusive of promotional space and displays.) And given that changes to store space allocation and positions can be expensive and disruptive, changes to stores should be tested in the market before rolling out to the entire chain. Which means that space is perhaps the least responsive lever that a retailer can use to change business patterns. (See the illustration below.) Consequently, for many retailers, space measurements and making changes to space is one of the least developed areas in the company.

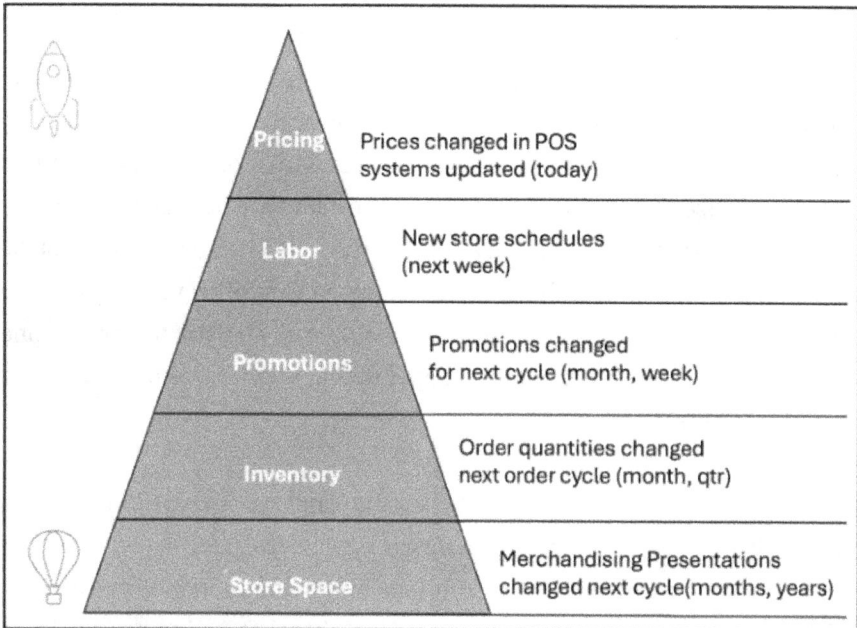

Figure 23: The difference in execution speed for retailers who need to make changes to drive business outcomes.

Space metrics are a new lens to merchandising information. For category managers who are used to looking at data at a category level, it adds complexity in ways that they may have never considered before. For example, most merchants are used to reviewing sales levels for items based on the number of stores carrying the product. And they may also contrast that with out-of-stock levels to identify upside opportunities. But when you then overlay planogram data that includes facings, shelf depth and location, the data becomes much richer – and more convoluted. It takes more time to analyze than a simple comparison. Stores start to change their productivity index locations when merchants have to consider the placement and shelf capacity for across all stores. Planogram data and space metrics can become so distinctive that common analysis tools like Tableau or BI sets built by category management practitioners don't deliver the proper insights. It is another reason that space analytics is often a stand-alone function.

For retailers who have an omnichannel strategy, space measurements don't tell the whole story. Merchants who are trying to satisfy omnichannel shoppers need to balance space metrics with overall inventory productivity metrics when orders are fulfilled from DC's or dark stores. And as retailers try to optimize their profits, separating the causality between changes in prices, promotions, displays and e-commerce from changes in space can be insurmountable. No merchant can be expected to synthesize such diverse reporting. Therefore, retailers often consolidate all analytic teams into one enterprise team who can combine all operational measurements into a more holistic scorecard.

Each retailer will have to look at their internal resources, toolsets and bandwidth to decide how they want to introduce space scorecards and measurements into their category plans and evaluations. What is most critical is that space measurements yield insights that lead to new business decisions. It makes no difference if a category manager finds out that that Brand A has a GMROS of $2.15 while Brand B has a GMROS of $4.59 if they do not know what they should do differently based on that measurement. (hint: All things being equal, give some of Brand A's space to Brand B.)

But organizationally, there is a choice for each retailer to determine whether space analytics will be conducted within the space planning team by space planning analysts. Or whether space analytics should be one of many levers that an enterprise-level analytic team manages. Amongst the things to consider is where expertise can be best recruited and developed. Too often space planning teams create an isolated group of data scientists or analysts who contribute an incredible amount to the company. But their leadership cannot give them the exposure and development they need to have a fulfilling and challenging career. So then, there are pros and cons to both approaches.

Keeping space analytics within the space planning team:

Pros	Cons
Understands the root causes behind the details of space data.	May not have the confidence of merchants and executives in a data reporting role.
Can make space-based recommendations to improve performance	May not be adept at integrating data across multiple sources to provide a single lens to view the business. Just reports on space – leaving it to others to integrate the findings and recommendations.

Placing space analytics within an enterprise-level team:

Pros	Cons
Generally respected and trusted across the company to provide insights and accurate reporting.	May be too far removed from space planning to explain data anomalies or detailed root causes.
The standard and expected source for information across the company. May have already established business cadences.	May not be adept at guiding better business decisions with space data. May default to other (pricing, inventory, etc.) levers.
Adept at knitting together disparate data sources into a unified report and recommendation.	May need attention and coaching from the space planning team.

A Space Planner's Career Path

It is fascinating to talk with space planning leaders and learn how they arrived in their role. In over thirty years, I have never heard a person say that they dreamed of being a space planner when they were a kid. Or that they went to college to become a space planner. Which is different from supply chain analysts or category merchants. Space planning seems to be an unintended career choice. One that came about through a series of choices and defaults that led to the realization that they are "good at space planning" or that they like the work. So, until there are college programs that intentionally create space planners, let's talk about how the space planner's career is likely to develop.

First, floor planners often have a more predictable career progression that often began with some level of CAD and architectural or construction design. Their focus early in their careers may have already been on how to design spaces and how people move through spaces. But it is the overlay of merchandising and analysis that separates an outstanding floor planner from a reasonably good layout designer. Thus, floor planners tend to be more analytic than their interior designing counterparts. Floor planners often had assignments in construction, new store design, and real estate. It is possible to find CAD specialists in technical colleges and train them to become floor planners. And, of course, if they are interested and apply themselves, it is possible to source good store planners from the field organization.

Planogrammers take a more circuitous route, usually. Many began either on the inventory transition team where they had to work closely with the planogram team to coordinate assortment changes or in the stores where they had responsibility for executing planogram changes. It isn't unusual to hear of a merchandising execution team member fed up with the "crazy planogram changes" pushed to the stores wanting to join the planogram team just to understand how such non-intuitive merchandising gets created. Frankly, those can be some of the best talents on the team.

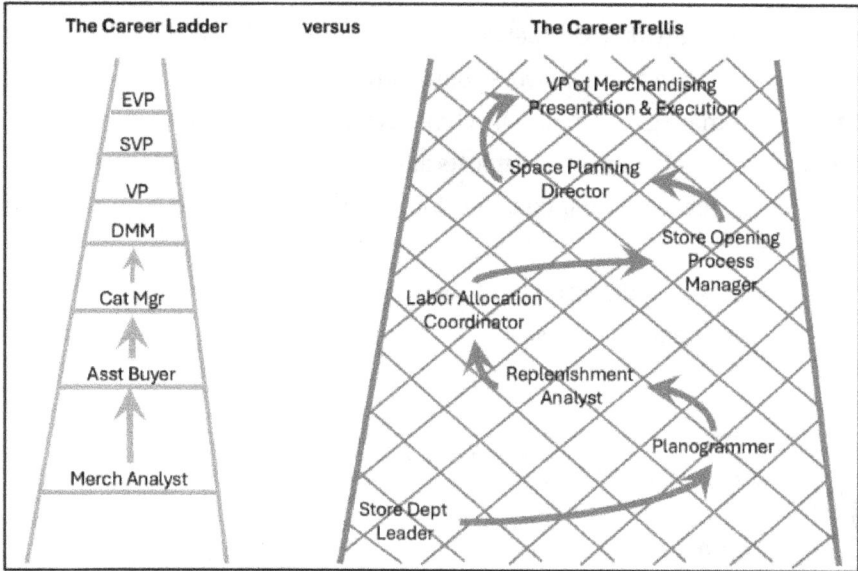

Figure 24: Career Trellises offer many ways to advance a career with many different experiences. Career ladders focus on a single functional expertise

Ideally, a planogrammer understands the category management process and how shopper insights are turned into relevant assortments and then applies those assortments to the fixture constraints that exist for each planogram. If they are also aware of the inventory allocation and replenishment process, store execution SOP's and are adept at using systems and computers, that is ideal. For planogrammers to enjoy their jobs, they have to be able to appreciate a focus on details. For planogrammers, the constant striving for complete, accurate, on time plans means that they must get a certain amount of satisfaction from following a process that yields repeatable results. A planogrammer who wanted to expand their role to creatively merchandise each planogram uniquely or who wanted to impose their own ideas over a category manager's guidance would not last long. For many planogrammers the joy comes from "making everything fit" while also completing their work on time. It can be a game like the sliding tile puzzle below.

Finally, space planners need to enjoy succeeding as a team. This is not a career where individual competition as a motivator helps achieve quotas and reach goals. Space planners work cooperatively with a diverse set of partners in category management, supply chain, store management and systems to succeed. A focus on smooth handoffs and reliable transitions is how a space planner can measure their contribution. Communications and camaraderie are almost second nature to the best space planners. If they are more cut out for winning and standing out and above others, they will create disruptions that will ripple across teams.

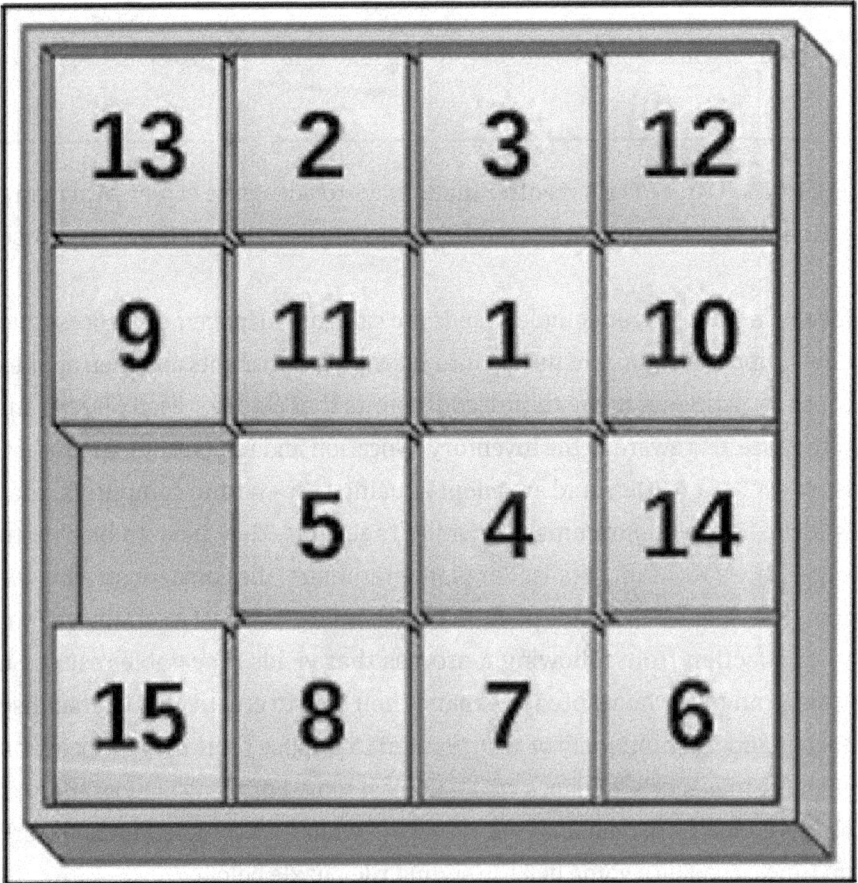

Figure 25: a tile sliding puzzle.

Winners Keep Score

With such a spirit of cooperation, you might wonder how a space planning team or individual can be evaluated. But space planning teams are regularly sized up using process metrics, accuracy metrics as well as resource productivity measurements.

The most common measurements evaluate whether a space planner is producing the quantity and quality of work within the expected time frame. Most organizations have an elaborate process schedule built around a "T-Minus" calendar which documents milestones that need to be reached to achieve a new store opening, remodel or planogram change on a scheduled date. Retailers have adopted the T-Minus countdown of rocket launches to indicate the launch of a new program or event in their stores.

There are T-minus milestones that need to be reached for a smooth store event. The T-minus refers to the number of weeks prior to the event. For example:

T-40	Vendors provide new item information & recommendations
T-38	Marketing Research provides shopper insights and trends. Category Managers begin vendor negotiations.
T-35	Category Managers hand over their recommended assortments by store types, market or size.
T-32	Space Planning reviews first draft planograms and validates merchandising changes.
T-30	Category managers make final assortment changes. Handoff to space planning. Vendor negotiations complete.
T-27	Final Planograms approved by Category Managers. Review final forecasts for new items and begin new item/vendor setup.
T-25	Clearance markdowns begin. Turn off replenishment for discontinued items. Incremental fixture order complete
T-24	All new item set up complete. Distribution Center slots procured. Review labor plan for T-0 week.
T-20	All new items forecasts complete. All new items ordered. New Signs ordered.
T-8	Labor scheduled for T-0 Implementation
T-4	New items arrive in DC. New Fixtures ship to stores. New shelf strips and signs ship to stores.
T-2	Planograms publish to stores.
T-1	All products arrive in stores. Clearance product moved to clearance locations.
T-0	Execute in stores.
T+1	Execution review/walk through and punch list.

This example can be compressed or expanded for each individual organization, but once set, it is rigid. Retailers base it on critical elements for their unique operation. Some retailers have deep private label or exclusive brand selections. They may require many months for new product formulation, production development, packaging and importing which adds weeks or months to the process. Others may have very fast turning items where clearance does not need to begin until T-4. Some retailers can deploy labor with very short notice while others may contract with third parties that require many weeks to prepare document and test.

But largely, space planning has key milestones in the T-minus countdown because it is the items assigned to a planogram and that planogram's assignment to a store that officially authorizes an item-to-store relationship. Meaning that a category manager can decide to eliminate an item that was previously carried in all stores to just the largest stores or just the stores in a particular cluster. That item is not discontinued from the inventory plan, nor is it eliminated in the distribution center. It is the planogram for small, medium and large stores that will determine how many and which specific stores that item will be found. Some stores will have to move the item to clearance, while others will continue replenishing it as normal.

Space planners are usually measured on whether or not they have hit their dates in a T-Minus calendar and delivered the draft and final planograms on time. This is a process metric. There is an internal process or handoff that is defined, and the space planners have to complete their portion of that handoff on time. The same kind of T-Minus, cross-functional calendar exists for opening new stores, remodeling or relocating a store and for reflowing the merchandise inside a store. Space planning leaders can hold their team accountable to the T-minus calendar by measuring their delivery of key handoff dates.

Other metrics have to do with the quality of the work. For floor planning, it means that every single business line that is expected for a store has a planned home location. There are critical adjacencies that are necessary to always maintain while others are more optional. Anchor businesses need to have specific placement, no matter the store footprint or prototype. Store changes are so expensive and disruptive, that floor plans are usually reviewed by many people before they are passed on to fixture vendors, construction contractors and field operations. But a store's plan is evaluated against baseline criteria for the project to measure the floor plan's completion and accuracy.

For planogrammers, there are usually merchandising standards and guidelines that are used to evaluate the accuracy and quality of their work. (For an example, see the Appendix.) The elements in merchandising standards can be focused on:

- Shopper and employee safety. For example: no glass bottles above 48" from the floor or no items stacked more than 1 high on the top shelf.
- Shelf space and inventory productivity. For example: cap all boxes to within 2" of the shelf above to maximize inventory capacity or no more than three items on a 9" peg to reduce inventory costs.
- Operational efficiency. For example: all items must have shelf capacity equal to or greater than 1.5 cases on the shelf.
- Visual appeal. For example: shelf heights must be held to a constant height from section to section across the entire planogram.

In addition to being reviewed for assortment transition accuracy (discontinued items are removed, new items are added), planograms are evaluated to ensure that they are meeting the retailer's merchandising standards.

Finally, planograms and floor layouts are measured for their contribution toward performance improvements. The high cost of making changes in stores is expected to return more sales, more profits and higher shopper satisfaction. For retailers, the proxy for meeting shopper needs is seeing increased revenue and unit sales. So, planograms and new store layouts are reviewed to see if they support a forecasted sales improvement prior to implementation. Then, after the store change occurs, they are evaluated through normal business reviews to ensure that they delivered the planned improvements. For more, read Chapter 7, Analyzing: Mastering the Science.

Space planning teams and individuals are measured by process metrics, standards and criteria and performance improvements. Measuring teams across these areas, allows a leader to understand how their organization is changing over time. Internally. They can see areas that are over- or under-indexing versus the balance of the team. But it cannot provide the kind of external benchmarking that most executives want to see. For cross-industry insights and comparisons, there are very few resources. Delaney Consulting is one specialized company that regularly measures and tracks those kinds of standards. A Space Planning community on LinkedIn is another resource.

Soft Skills - Mastering The Relationships

I f ever there was a functional area defined as "influencing without authority," it is space planning. Whether at a retailer or a supplier, the space planning team constantly feels pulled by the competing pressures of merchants, stores, supply chain, operations, promotions and shopper satisfaction. One of the best things about space planning is that it is at the center of the action. The work in space planning makes a huge difference to many people. That can also be one of the worst things about space planning. Accordingly, to succeed and have a long career, space planners must be skillful in building and nurturing relationships.

While there are some decisions that space planners can make, they tend to pale in comparison to strategic choices others make around product selection, market positioning and timelines. Unskilled communicators can burn out quickly in a space planning role as they try to navigate competing priorities and high impact demands. On both sides of the desk, space planners can take back more control and find higher job satisfaction when they focus on the soft skills more than remaining heads down on a keyboard.

Here are the soft skills that successful space planners demonstrate:

Relationship building – build trust and rapport with your colleagues, partners and stakeholders. In the continuum between relationship and results, always seek balance.

<u>Listen for understanding</u> – Actively listen and demonstrate that you both hear and value other people's opinions. When someone suggests something, you clearly disagree with, stop and say, "tell me more about that." Then reply with "so what you're saying is...." to show you listened well. If you still disagree with them, ask questions like "Have you considered....? How would you prioritize....?" Once you understand what motivates the person sitting across from you, you can find ways to build bridges from your motivation to theirs.

<u>Demonstrate competence</u> – A boss I worked with long ago held a title three or four levels higher than mine. I felt lucky just to be in the same room as people at his level during meetings. So, it was pretty terrifying when he would single me out to provide recommendations about what to do when a thorny merchandising problem came up. I swallowed and stammered my way through a response hedging everything I said in case I was wrong. Later he took the time to address everyone seeing how unnaturally respectful I was being. He said,

"Leadership flows to the expert in the room. Not the title of anyone in the room."

What he meant was that despite anyone's title, if you have the demonstrated competence to be the expert on *that one thing*, then you are the expert in the room for the moment. It is rare that there are many space planning experts in any given business meeting. Even if your job grade is not the highest in the room, when the topic turns to space planning and you are the acknowledged expert on it, you can influence without authority.

<u>Patience and Adaptability</u> – Easy to say. Difficult to acquire. But building influence takes time. You will have to build a reputation for being a solid contributor and a reliable partner to gain trust. Be patient with yourself and just as forgiving of others as you are with yourself.

Act on feedback – First, ask and be open to feedback. Demonstrate that you want to hear what other people think you could do better or what they value in you. Then, listen and adjust your approach when you can.

There are many books written on how to lead, influence and develop soft skills. As a leader in space planning, it is more common to see soft skills hold back a talented colleague than technical skills like whether they can key bind a programmable mouse to bulk move a section on a floor plan. Pay attention to the soft skills and your career will thank you.

Applying Soft Skills: A day in the life

Here are several common issues that occur with space planners and how proper soft skills can help navigate rough waters:

Last minute and late changes to the assortment

By far, this is the most common complaint heard from planogrammers about their category management partners. When this happens (and it is when – not if) take a pause and ask about the root cause. Find out why it happened. Is your CM new? Did the supplier provide a last-minute change? Are processes not understood? If you don't know why it happened, it is impossible to prevent it from happening again. In the thick of it, the sad fact is that 90% of the time, you will just have to adjust and get the work done with the late hand off.

But suggest that the cross-functional team take a few moments and conduct a 5-Why analysis.

The 5-why analysis is a particular approach that helps organizations get to the underlying cause of an issue. It is called 5-why because for each time that there is an answer, the next step is to ask, "why that happened." It goes like this:

The situation: The Lighting category assortment was turned over to space planning a week late. To make the necessary planogram changes, the team will have to rush and reprioritize the work ahead of other planned category changes.

Why did the CM process the final assortment past our due date?

Answer: The CM knew from past experience that if they had a good reason for a late assortment turnover, that the space planning team could accommodate a delayed final assortment.

Why did the final assortment change?

Answer: There was a vendor who increased their prices which meant that some of the items the CM originally planned to put into the selection had to be reviewed a second time. Some of the original items were not approved.

Why did we not know about the price changes earlier?

Answer: We ask vendors to provide their pricing in their original submission that occurs 3 months before assortment selection and sometimes their pricing changes in the interim and we do not know.

Why didn't the vendor tell us about the pricing change?

Answer: Vendors have no way to edit their original submissions on our portal until they receive an "approved" item status so they cannot review or change their final pricing and terms until then.

Why don't we allow vendors to edit prices in their submission?

Answer: We decided we had to "lock" our new item submissions 90 days out from selection so our CMs would have time to make choices about what to carry.

So here is an example where the fundamental reason for a late hand off was a rule in place on a vendor portal. Perhaps there would be an interest in changing the process for vendors. Or a change to the editable fields. Or the timing for lockdown that is closer to the selection. But the point is that by doing a 5-why analysis, there is a greater understanding of the root cause of the delay. Thus, providing more empathy towards everyone involved as it seemed like so many parties (the vendor, the CM, the space team) simply got caught in a situation that was a bit out of their hands.[9]

Construction dates getting pushed back

If late assortment handoffs are the bane of the planograming team, construction date delays are the number one complaint from floor planners. There are so many reasons why a planned new store or remodel can be delayed. Usually, it involves securing necessary permits and tradespeople in time, passing inspections, materials arriving on time, unreliable deliveries from transportation companies, or having the labor ready for a project.

So first and foremost, absolutely expect that project timing for stores will change. If you can modify your expectations for store projects to understand that dates are tentative until they happen, you can put yourself and your team in the right headspace to adjust for those inevitable delays and changes. When you reduce your own stress over changes, you give yourself space to react properly – and without frustration. How do you do that? Have a routine SOP for adjusting store project timing that accounts for all the cross-functional touchpoints that need to be informed of a change.

Let's review examples of the kinds of cross-functional problems that can

---

9   Although I might advise the CM to place a call to the vendor to ask them to reach out via email or phone call whenever a new item has a price change prior to final item selection.

occur when a project is delayed with this Midtown Mall store case. The Midtown Mall stores was going to have a major remodel on October 1st. In the remodel, the First Aid section was going to shrink from 12' to 6' and the Oral Care section was going to increase from 12' to 18'. To support that change, the pricing team had started to discount first aid items on August 1 to clear them out of the store's inventory in advance of the change. The inventory team had stopped replenishing those items to Midtown as they sold down.

The inventory team had also started to build inventory in the warehouse for the additional items Midtown Mall would carry in Oral Care. They were planning to ship them to the store on September 20th.

If the delay was decided on September 1st, the First Aid items could perhaps revert to their original prices. But the inventory team would need to decide whether to start replenishing those items to possibly mark them down again in the future. Or to allow the store to operate with out of stocks in the first aid section. In any case, there was an unnecessary profit margin leak on those products. Meanwhile, the warehouse turn on oral care will slow down because the plan was to ship an initial allocation out on September 20th. That is not dangerous to the company's health, but it is another unnecessary drain on capital.

Finally, the store operators in the Midtown Mall store are making changes to pricing labels and responding to customers asking about the first aid products they want that are out of stock. To be honest, they are being truthful when they tell customers they don't know if or when the items will be back in stock.

When store projects get delayed there are two critical things that need to happen:

1. Revert the store record to the old floorplan so that planogram assign-ments are correct. Usually this is done by placing the planned floorplan into a suspended status and reviewing the previous floorplan version to

make sure that it will be operational until the project can resume.

2. Do not delete or overwrite the suspended floorplan. That floorplan probably needs to have a new LIVE date applied to it and needs to be updated when it goes live. This is especially true if there are designated planograms or seasonal products that are applied to the floorplan.

In our earlier example of the Midtown Mall store, the project was supposed to go live on October 1. Let's say the delay pushes that date to January 15. Before the suspended floorplan goes live in January, all of the Halloween seasonal sections need to be updated with Valentine's Day products. There could be other necessary changes to keep it up to date. But you get the picture. That floorplan cannot just go on ice and then be reissued when it is executed.

To keep everyone apprised, make sure your company has a proper working team meeting or at least a group email that inform everyone affected by a change. (including the store management team!)

Stores did not execute or provided negative feedback on merchandising direction.

This can appear in many ways. Like when you are on a market visit with other team members or executives, and you are asked to defend a store condition that is clearly not merchandised as planned. Maybe there are a few store or district managers who reliably complain about the merchandising direction they're sent. Maybe you have seen too many backrooms with the signs gathering dust rather than on display on the sales floor. Maybe you see broken fixtures or displays when you have sent dozens of reminders to stores about how to repair or replace them. Probably, on any given week, it is all of the above.

Here's the thing about having empathy for people who run and merchandise the stores. While you are earnest in your focus to help them have a beautifully merchandised store that operates efficiently, they have other priorities. Most of the time, they are dealing with complications that we don't even consider. Like cashiers and backroom receivers not showing up for a shift. Which means that the team members who were scheduled for merchandising have to spend their shift at the checkout. Or a mandatory health inspection for the fresh food departments that requires all hands-on deck to ensure that every food handling location is up to code. Or a shoplifting theft that requires interviews with police and the shopping mall security team. A fight in the parking lot, a disposal contractor not unloading the dumpster, a rush on the store in advance of a storm, a complaint on social media that blew up. There are so many other things that may happen in the course of operating a store. Keep that in mind to give your merchandising issues some balance and keep it in proportion. That does not mean store teams are unaccountable for the store's conditions. It just means to approach the issue from a place of understanding.

The best way to do that is to "seek first to understand." Your success, a store's success, the company's success: it is all interdependent. For that reason, first ask how you could help them succeed in whatever you believe is substandard to start. Listen and re-center the conversation on how to help them succeed. If you hear the same complaint from more than one store or more than a few times, there is probably something to the complaint. Try to keep from becoming deaf to an excuse you have heard before. Build trust. Take action. Even if the action doesn't relieve the situation, let them know that they are heard, and you are trying to make improvements. Make sure you think about the store manager who works in a market and only hears from the HQ is when there is a problem. That's not a great feeling. With every store visit, make sure you thank them for their time and find an authentic feature you can compliment.

More than anything, get to know the store teams as people. As well as you know your own team, if possible. Visit stores. Remember people in the stores and work your own resets. It is one of the best ways to identify problems with your merchandising plans while they are still in the planning phase and build trust and credibility with your store team.

Executives or other departments ask for information you cannot provide.

For people who do not work in space planning, the information at your fingertips can sometimes seem limitless. Because from their vantage point, Space planners know every item's location in every store. They know how much time it will take to make a merchandising change. They know the adjacencies for every category and which ones improve sales. And in a way - they are sort of right. Certainly, all those things are know-*able* with clean and complete space planning data. But it is a rare retailer who has every item in each store planogrammed. For reasons we have already mentioned, fashion, perishable and seasonal items are regularly not planogrammed. And if space plans are produced for sets of stores (not individual stores) then things like adjacencies can only be presumed correct unless the retailer has a robust monitoring system.

Every time a partner asks for data that they believe the space planning team has, is a chance to educate and prioritize future work. First, be direct in telling them that the exact information that they asked for is not something you can provide. But quickly follow that with an inquiry about what they are attempting to find out to see if there is some other way you can triangulate on a solution. Explain what is missing and why you cannot provide the information as they asked for it. If it is a lack of store-specific planograms, missing foundational data, incomplete visibility for certain departments, etc. be clear. Ask for their advocacy to have their issue known and raised to the leaders or teams that could improve the situation. Then work with the person to investigate other proxy information that you can provide.

What is important is to not just state "No, we don't have that." And leave them hanging. Every partner that you have to say "no" to is a person you could transform into an advocate for space planning. Explain to them what it would take to be able to give them exactly what they want and ask them to take the message to others they may be able to influence. Suggest jointly prioritizing requests for resources to demonstrate the power of combining multiple user groups.

In the game of career progression and job satisfaction, remember that your joy will come from two places: doing your job well and doing it with people you like. Being competent is most certainly table stakes in your career. But how well you are liked and get along with the people you are around each day will be the root of your perseverance and purpose.

Network your Way to Career Success

As you build your career you will need to have a strong network of people who are straight shooters with you. Whether you move up internally with promotions or seek new challenges with new companies, it is key to have connections who advocate for you and help coach you through career decisions. Maybe you have a large flourishing network. Maybe the concept of the verb "networking" makes your stomach turn. But if you can't or won't nurture people who matter to you, don't expect them to do much for you when the time comes.

In this industry, there are regular cycles of change. Departments get built and staff up. Then economic cycles change and downsizes happen. No matter how secure you feel, it is always a good idea to have a healthy network just in case. You cannot ignore people for years and then expect to pick up the phone when you find a new opportunity they could help you with.

So then, as a career space planner it is important to build and cultivate a network of people that will help you as you make choices about your career. Let's examine how to do that:

Rule #1: You have to care. Care about people and genuinely want to keep the people that you have worked with, volunteered with or hung out with in a positive place in your life. Have you ever felt abandoned when close work friends move on to new companies and you never hear from them again? Look closely at how you behave once you move out of a circle of people. Do you assume that since you "don't have much going on" that they don't want to hear from you? Your relationships grew out of those convenient opportunities to grab lunch or a cup of coffee on average days on the job. If you want to keep people in your network, you must create those opportunities now by picking up the phone or texting and letting them know you still want to get together. If you honestly want to keep the relationship, you will find the time.

Rule #2: EVERYONE IS BUSY. Yeah, you are busy. I know. No one is sitting by the phone. But when it rings isn't it nice when it's someone you enjoyed talking to in the past and they called to see how you are doing and to set up time to get together? Of course, it is. And you may have to schedule two or three months out to make it work - but keep that appointment and you have gone a long way to helping people know they are a priority with you. Because it isn't about being busy - it's about *priorities*. Make keeping your network alive a priority. Of course, you should not prioritize your work friends above your child's ball game or concert. But isn't it more important than binging the latest streaming series or playing games on your phone?

If you start out with these intentions, here are some good habits to develop to make your network flourish:

1. Use technology to help you cheat at being good with people. Consider the NOTES section of Outlook. Make a couple of notes in Outlook when you talk to members of your network: The date you last spoke or saw them, names of spouses, kids or pets, favorite sports teams, vacation spots, anything that will jog your memory the next time that you speak to them and let them know that you listen, and you care. You'll score plenty of points when you ask how their trip to Aspen was or if Snickers is house trained yet.

2. Make a weekly goal to call 5 people in your network by Friday. Go through your contacts and select the easy ones first. Give yourself 15 minutes a day to do it. To be honest, you'll leave a lot of voice mails. But if you can just reconnect with a couple each week, you will prevent your network from declining. This single action taken for a few weeks will absolutely change how connected you feel with your network. If you are unsure of what to say, here are some opening lines:

"I was just going through my contacts and saw your name and knew I had to call you just to check in. Dang, I miss you!"

"I was just thinking how we used to see each other nearly every day working on project X and I miss that. Not the project - just talking. Want to get together?"

"Susie Q asked about you the other day and I was caught flat-footed because I realized it's been ages since I saw you. How are you doing?"

1. Coffee, Lunch, Beers, Taco Bell runs. All are great excuses to get together with someone from your network. If you work from home or eat alone, you are in danger of becoming caught in repetitive thought patterns. Put some change into your life by inviting someone you like but don't see enough to join you.

2. Insert this into EVERY networking conversation: "What can I do to help you?" Seems simple, but it's a sentence that carries great meaning and can open up your conversation in a whole new way. They may be looking for a new babysitter, wondering about a strange sound in their engine block or how to ask for a raise. Whatever it may be, listen and then follow up and DO whatever you have committed to. Usually it is easy: look at my resume, ask me to lunch again, listen to me tell you about my recent bad day. But I guarantee that saying this sentence will make you and them feel better. (Oh, and by rule of reciprocity, there is often something they would like to do for you as well.)

3. Use LinkedIn. There are a gaggle of other applications to use as well, but to be taken seriously, LinkedIn is the granddaddy of them all. Join one of the several Space Planning groups on Linkedin and start following conversations. When you are serious about networking, start participating in comments and create threads. It's a great way to make a name for yourself in the industry. Not sure how to connect: find my profile on LinkedIn and ask to connect. Tell me you read this book, and I will always agree. Then you will be connected to my network. Boom!

4. Make some tough calls. You know the ones I mean. After a month or two of calling your pals, it's time to reach out to some of those people who you have ignored for a while. First bosses, first employees, people who helped make you who you are today and that you have lost touch with. It feels hard to do, but there are two things that will make it easier:

They are going to be THRILLED to hear from you. After all this time, you'll find that all they really want to know is that you are doing okay and that you remember them well. You are and you do.

You will feel terrific about reaching out and reconnecting. That little bit of guilt you have for not being the one to call will go away and you will want to repeat it again with your newly expanding network.

Your network can be as large as the international community of space planners or as small as the people on your immediate team. The point is, you need a group of people who know you and who you can use as reliable sounding boards for the ups and downs of your work life. You do not need a network filled with Vice Presidents and people who can help you get places. You need a network of people who know your strengths and your opportunities and are comfortable enough with you to tell you the truth. That is the power of a network - no matter the size.

To really amp up your networking skills, be in the right frame of mind to meet with people. Just take a few minutes to get prepared. I like to be prepared by just saying 4 words to myself. "Be Kind. Be Generous" If you repeat those words before entering a conversation, you can be ready to do what is most important: listen.

When I say, "be kind," I mean it in two ways. Be nice to people like wait staff, janitors and receptionists. It matters. And it is one of the prime ways people evaluate whether you are well bred. The other way is to be kind with your time. Be generous in giving time to people who may not be able to "help you" but may need some guidance and advice from your experience. These folks may be tiresome at times because the career challenges they face are ones you may have decided on years ago or they mean very little to you. Make time to listen and you will be surprised at the impact you can have on other people. After all, in a network you must be willing to help others as much as you might want help.

Be generous means listening to what is happening with them and support the needs they have. Maybe they just need someone to listen. Or they genuinely need advice on a tricky situation. If you are giving, they will want to be connected to you frequently. They will also feel compelled to be equally generous when you need something, That's human nature.

Another way to be generous is to regularly forward relevant information to your network. It can be as breezy as a text that says "you must be walking on air after that Giants win last night" or as serious as forwarding an article you read on changing household spending. The point is, when you read something that strikes you as interesting, ask yourself who else in your network might also want to hear that. Being relevant is easy if you tap into a few industry newsletters, blogs or podcasts. Plus, it makes an easy way to reach out to people without having to find a creative excuse.

But as you are networking, be discreet. Avoid a reputation for gossiping or your network will dwindle quickly and not be the professional support and guidance you are looking for at all. People will value you if they know they can discuss sensitive items with you, and you will be a Fort Knox with their concerns. Learn to graciously turn away people seeking "dirt" by saying things like "Oh, I don't want to talk about Brad or Marketing. Tell me what is new with you." When the topic starts to veer into gossip, just say "Oh that makes me tired" then change the subject.

To make networking second nature, stop keeping score. Honestly, that may be the most difficult thing about networking since it goes against the way we are wired for reciprocity. If you value a relationship that has gone cold through email or otherwise, do not assume the person meant to end it. In other words, if you are waiting because, "you communicated last and now it's their turn," get over yourself. Pick up the phone and text or when you get their voice mail (because if they are too busy to return your emails, they are probably too busy to answer the phone) use your cheerful voice to say you miss them and want to set up time soon to get together and then offer a few dates and times. Chances are, when they hear you are not looking for them to do something or are reminding them that they "owe" you a response, they will be more inclined to reply. There are times when we all get more than we give. Cut them a break and be the bigger person who stops keeping score.

Another key to networking is to find your pack. By that, I mean the other space planning experts in the industry. Every space planner I know craves finding other people who understand their challenges and dedication to the practice. The space planning community is not so large. There are ways to connect outside of your company through LinkedIn groups, user conferences for the software you use and through webinars and hosted events. If you can make just one connection and nurture it, you can create a safe place to ask questions and figure out if other people faced with the same challenges you have, resolved it in a new way. For space planning leaders, having a trusted circle of experts who will answer the phone when you call is key to staying on top of industry trends and finding great candidates when jobs are available.

If you are wondering where to start, consider connecting to me on LinkedIn.

Sure, why not? You bought the book – don't I owe you something? And once you are connected to me, you will see hundreds of other space planners in my network. All there for you to tap into and network. It's the least I can do...

The life of a space planner is busy. There are deadlines and new crises every day. But for space planners who build a career that they are proud of, having a strong network both inside and outside their company is a key. It is never too late to start. Like building new muscles at the gym, your first attempts will be feeble and make you feel uncomfortable. But the key to success at the gym isn't what you do at the gym. It's getting to the gym. Just show up. For yourself and your co-workers.

Appendix

What every space planner should know:

E very space planning system installation is different and used differently. But to be proficient in your installation, make sure you can answer the following questions. Ask a more seasoned space planner on your team if you need assistance. Here are 43 questions you should be able to answer within your own system to be proficient.

How do I.....

...add a new item?

...change a shelf to another micro article?

...turn on squeeze/crush for many items at once?

...check to see if squeeze/crush is turned on?

...add a new segment to the left?

...add a new segment to the right?

...change the size of a segment?

...create a text box or placeholder?

...save my work?

...promote a planogram to a new status?

...check to see which stores have a planogram?

...check to see if there is a minimum of 1 case on the shelf?

...change the dimensions of a product?

...change the dimensions of a shelf?

...add vertical facings for all products on a shelf?

...reduce vertical facings for all products on a shelf?

...set a shelf in a notch?

...change my bottom information ribbon on my screen?

...give feedback?

...open a help ticket?

...find shortcuts?

...open more than 1 planogram at once?

...copy and paste across planograms

...zoom in?

...zoom out?

...return to center front view?

...change my performance data?

...export to excel?

...print a pdf?

...AutoNumber my shelves?

...change my slatwall or pegboard spacing?

...change the space between pegs on a slatwall or pegboard?

...change the length of a peg hook?

...change a highlight field?

...report a missing image?

...change product labels?

....change shelf labels?

...print with highlights on?

...print with labels on?

...change product orientation?

...change product orientation for many products at once?

...drag many items onto my shelf at once?

...disco many items from my POG at once?

Off Cycle Planogram Change Pro Forma Template - Blank

Today's date   _____
Date of Requested POG Change   _____
Date of next scheduled POG change   _____
Number of months difference*   _____

Current sales/month (12 mo avg)   _____
Current margin % /month   _____
Current margin $ / month   _____

Projected new sales per month   _____
Projected margin % /month   _____
Projected new margin $ / month   _____

Projected new monthly margin $ increase   _____
Projected total margin $ for duration*   _____
Number of planograms affected   _____
Projected production hours per POG   _____
Avg POG production cost/hour   _____
Total projected POG Production cost   _____

Number of stores affected   _____
Projected POG set hours per store   _____
Average hourly wage estimate   _____
Total projected POG set cost   _____

Off cycle duration benefit   _____
Off cycle costs   _____
Net results   _____

Signoffs: Space planning, Category Management, Retail Operations, etc. See next page.

Off Cycle Planogram Change Pro Forma Template – filled out

Today's date	7/25/2024
Date of Requested POG Change	10/15/2024
Date of next scheduled POG change	1/15/2025
Number of months difference*	3
Current sales/month (12 mo avg)	$50,000.00
Current margin % /month	32.5%
Current margin $ / month	$16,250.00
Projected new sales per month	$52,000.00
Projected margin % /month	34.5%
Projected new margin $ / month	$17,940.00
Projected new monthly margin $ increase	$1,690.00
Projected total margin $ for duration*	$5070.00
Number of planograms affected	6
Projected production hours per POG	4 hrs
Avg POG production cost/hour	$50.00/hr
Total projected POG Production cost	$1200.00
Number of stores affected	80
Projected POG set hours per store	6 hrs
Average hourly wage estimate	$16.00/hr
Total projected POG set cost	$7680.00
Off cycle duration benefit	$5,070.00
Off cycle costs	$8,881.00
Net results	($3811.00)

Signoffs: Space planning, Category Management, Retail Operations, etc.

In this example, the change is likely to be denied. Note that the category manager or the financial planner provides the estimates, the space planning team provides the planogram component estimates, and the store operations team provides the store execution estimates.

Sample Systems Interface Diagram

A Sample of Merchandising Guidelines

Strategic Guidelines

1. We will create a shoppable, consistent and efficient experience for customers and store associates balancing the breadth and depth of our selection with the holding power needed for operational considerations.
2. We will protect core customers through our deep selection in our merchandising and capture occasional customer purchases by highlighting our opening price point products in a prominent "lead off" location in our planograms.
3. We will protect our private label brands by merchandising them in their appropriate brand block instead of scattering the brand and pairing each item with their similar national brand.

Visual Merchandising Guidelines:

1. We will follow customer decision tree guidance to organize our sets – whether by brand or by attribute based on how shoppers view substitutability for the category.
2. Within blocks of our presentation, products will be organized in a good>better>best alignment from a price/brand perspective.
3. Facing decisions will adhere to first (1) Case pack out – where our goal is that all products in a planogram will have a minimum of one full case pack out on the shelf and then (2) Holding Power – where our goal is that all items will have enough DOS on the shelf to meet one full delivery cycle plus 2 days of sales.
4. When we are space constrained to meet our goals above, we will use an assortment ranking to rationalize selection and reduce item counts in planograms.

Operational Guidelines:

1. Top Shelf – our top shelves are measured from the floor to be shoppable by our customers. Top shelves will be set no higher than 80" above the floor.
2. Bookending products (where items are rotated 90 degrees for fill a horizontal gap on the shelf.) Bookends will only be on the item on the furthest right of a shelf and should not be place in the middle of a shelf.
3. Capping (where a box is laid down to fill a vertical gap between an item and the shelf above it.) Not an approved merchandising style except on the bottom two shelves of a planogram. If there are large vertical air gaps between upper shelves, use the bottom two shelves to absorb that distance/gap. Target a 2" gap between shelves.
4. Stacking (placing items one upon the other in the width of a single facing.) Only boxes, cartons or cans may be stacked. Pouches, bottles, tubes may not be stacked.
5. Top Shelf:

· Glass bottles or jars may not be placed on the top shelf.
· NO items may be stacked on the top shelf.

1. Bottom Shelf:

· The bottom shelf is reserved for the highest cube items in the set. Items shorter than 9" are not recommended for placement on the bottom shelf (to reduce visual stockouts.)

1. Finger space (the minimum and maximum distance between the top of a product and the shelf above it.)

· Maximum vertical gap between a product and the shelf above it is 4". If the gap is >4", consider moving the product to a higher or lower shelve to maximize space efficiency and provide a better aesthetic representation for the category.
· Minimum finger space should be 1" especially where the product is

"locked" be a downward channel strip from the shelf above it making it difficult to shop. Consider greater finger space for packages that are heavy or bulky and require shoppers to grasp the package firmly before removing it from a shelf.

1. Value size/multi pack, full case products will be merchandised at 38" from the floor or below in order to make them safely accessible for shoppers.
2. Multiple locations

- Product will not be merchandised on multiple shelves unless days of supply (DOS) warrants multiple shelf placements of full shelves.
- Products on multiple peg hooks will be merchandised in vertical, rather than horizontal, groupings for as many as necessary to meet pack out/DOS requirements.

System Guidelines:

1. Stores will receive planograms that match their precise in-store conditions within +/- 4" in planogram height and +/- 2" in planogram width. Any obstruction, obstacle or floor planning element which violates these limits, will trigger an "planogram to build" for a new planogram version to accommodate the difference.
2. Planograms will not publish with:

- Items in the planogram file (backroom) that are not merchandised. All unmerchandised products must be removed from the final planogram file.
- Products or shelves that are "floating." All products and shelves must be anchored.
- "Flex" or "Store Discretion" space that exceeds more than 5% of the overall planogram cubic space. Except "closeout" endcaps and locations that are meant to reduce store-specific inventory excess.

- Text boxes, placeholders, TBD or other work arounds meant to stand in for items that have not been set up in the central product library.
- Split planograms and wrap around planograms (when a single POG must be merchandised across the aisle or wrapped around an endcap to the next aisle for very small stores) are only acceptable when the planogram remains within the department and all other adjacencies cannot be adjusted. Split planograms and wrap around planograms must be approved by the Space Planning Director prior to publishing.

Final checklist prior to publishing:

1. All Fixture IDs are correct and match the macro fixture on the floorplan. (check this by running XYZ report)
2. The base deck is 7" and the base shelf is 1.25" (product begins at 8.25" off the floor)
3. All pegged products have the proper peg type and length (single, double, locking, etc.)
4. All shelves are set to fill to the maximum Z depth of units.
5. All unallocated products have been removed using the "remove unallocated" command.
6. All segments are properly aligned to the gondola notches. View in 3D for visual reference.
7. View in 3D to verify product is not deeper than the shelf (sticking out the back) or in front of the shelf or peg hook.
8. All user-created fields have been returned to their previous values.
9. All dates are correct.
10. All products have images. Work with the product librarian to address issues.
11. POG meets the visual standards for the category.
12. The planogram has been reviewed by LP for any security measures to be addressed during execution.

Promotional Guidelines

1. Locations will be prioritized when a merchant can get immediate incremental sales.
2. Outposted locations will be prioritized when a new item can be tested without removing items from what is already planogramed in secondary locations.
3. Stores may not place additional locations/displays in their stores when it obstructs the ease of our customers shopping our aisles.

- All promotional planograms are set up to run in compliance with standard planogram replenishment. What that means, is that once the POG is in LIVE status and the store's floor plan is also in LIVE status, the product on that promotional planogram will replenish for the duration of the LIVE status of the promotional POG.

Recommended by the Author

To learn more about Retail and Space Planning, consider:

- Delaney, Flora. *The Space Planning Handbook.* Minneapolis: Waterford and Howell Publishing, 2024
- Delaney, Flora. *Retail: The Second-Oldest Profession, 7 Timeless Principles to WIN in Retail Today.* Minneapolis: Waterford and Howell Publishing, 2019
- King, David C. *Selling with Space Planning.* New York: Fairchild Publications, 1994

To improve your career, consider:

- Ferrazzi, Keith, and Tahl Raz. *Never Eat Alone: And Other Secrets to Success, One Relationship at a Time.* New York: Currency/Doubleday, 2005
- Stone, Douglas, Bruce Patton, and Sheila Heen. *Difficult Conversations: How to Discuss What Matters Most.* New York: Penguin Books, 1999

Want BONUS content?

www.Floradelaney.com/extras has exclusive BONUS MATERIAL on store operations, execution and Space Planning. It's just a way to say thank you for reading this book. And, if you wish, please leave us a review on Amazon, Goodreads or wherever you connect with other readers.

About the Author

F lora Delaney is a thought leader and expert in space planning, category management and merchandising. Her experience leading grocery, hardware, consumer electronics and other retailers give her a wealth of experience. Combined with IT solution insights and marketing savvy, her clients benefit from her guidance and advice. Flora is also an author of two other books: The Space Planning Handbook the companion book to this volume and Retail: The Second-Oldest Profession, 7 Timeless Principles to WIN in Retail Today released in 2019.

For a handy reference, keep *The Space Planning Handbook* nearby. It's the must-have reference for all retail space experts. A handy reference for data, fixtures, merchandising, resources and regulations that impact store layout and planogram experts. Includes a detailed 64-page glossary. Also contains exercises and knowledge checks to reinforce and customize industry standards for each reader.

Readers say:

It's like space planning 101 training in an easy-to-use handbook.

This is the book that should be on every planogrammer's desk. Such a great reference!

I turn to this book whenever I need to remember all the details that have grown fuzzy since my training.

A perfect overview of the basics of space planning and its technical specifications for any system.

Available on Amazon or wherever you go to get books. (We kind of hope it is a good ol' independent bookstore, to be honest.)

www.ingramcontent.com/pod-product-compliance
Lightning Source LLC
Chambersburg PA
CBHW071552210326
41597CB00019B/3209